Alexander Ferrier Mitchell

The Wedderburns and their work

The sacred poetry of the Scottish reformation in its historical relation to that of

Germany

Alexander Ferrier Mitchell

The Wedderburns and their work
The sacred poetry of the Scottish reformation in its historical relation to that of Germany

ISBN/EAN: 9783742862587

Manufactured in Europe, USA, Canada, Australia, Japa

Cover: Foto ©Thomas Meinert / pixelio.de

Manufactured and distributed by brebook publishing software
(www.brebook.com)

Alexander Ferrier Mitchell

The Wedderburns and their work

WEDDERBURNS AND THEIR WORK

OR

THE SACRED POETRY OF THE SCOTTISH REFORMATION IN ITS
HISTORICAL RELATION TO THAT OF GERMANY

A Lecture

BY ALEX. F. MITCHELL D.D.

PROFESSOR OF HEBREW, ST ANDREWS

"Concordes animæ, clarissima lumina genti
Tres paribus studii tæc pietate pares."

WILLIAM BLACKWOOD AND SONS
EDINBURGH AND LONDON.

MDCCCXVII.

JOHANNES WEDDERBVRNVS.

Pulsus in exilium, an. 1546. Exul in Anglia moritur 1556.

I.

Non meriti est nostri, meritas tibi dicere grates,
    Aut paria, aut aliqua parte referre vicem.
Quæ meruisse alii vellent, nec posse mereri est :
    Hæc velle, hæc posse, hæc te meruisse tuum est.
Sic facis atque canis sacra : sic agis omnia, nil ut
    Sanctius, et nusquam purior ulla fides.
Hinc nullum magis invisum caput hostibus : hinc et
    Nemo unquam meruit charior esse bonis.
Grandius hoc meritum, nil te meruisse fateris,
    Humanis meritis nec superesse locum.

II.

DE JOHANNE, JACOBO, ET ROBERTO WEDDERBVRNO, FRATRIBUS.

Divisum imperium, per tres, tria Numina, Fratres,
    Infera quæque vides, quæque superna, canunt.
Vos miror potius tres vero nomine fratres,
    Vosque supra veneror, Numina vana, Deos ;
Concordes animas, clarissima lumina gentis,
    Tres paribus studiis, tres pietate pares.
Felices qui vos tales genuere parentes,
    Quæque orbi tellus pignora rara dedit.
Progenitos Cælo Alectum dedit inclyta terris :
    Inde DEI-DONUM nomen habere putem.

JONSTONI, "περι Στεφανων."

(M'Crie's Life of Knox, p. 463.)

PREFACE.

The Lecture which follows is the substance of an introductory address prepared during last winter for the St Andrews Students' Missionary Society, and afterwards rewritten and delivered to a Young Men's Christian Association in Forfarshire. It is now printed very much in the form in which it was last delivered; but some notes and appendices, which seemed necessary for the farther illustration of the subject, have been added, and in Appendix IV. the original introduction to the address has been given at full length.

In the extracts adduced in the Lecture from the "Godly and Spiritual Songs," I have usually conformed to the modern practice in the use of *u* and *v*, and changed such antiquated Scotch forms as zow, ze, zet, into yow, ye, and yet; but in the extracts subjoined in the appendices I have left the words very much in the form in which they are found in Dalyell's reprint. In the extracts given from the old German hymns I have generally adhered to the words of Wackernagel's text; but in the spelling of the words I have generally conformed to a North German Hymn-book of 1636, which approaches far more nearly to the modern usage. I have not thought it necessary to print the German nouns with initial capitals, as Wackernagel has not done so, and Bunsen, in his Gesangbuch, has set the example of returning to the old practice: nor have I marked the omission of *e* final by an apostrophe, nor the abbreviation of sein for sein'n, ihr for ihr'r, &c., as the usage of Wackernagel in these respects is sanctioned in several modern hymn-books. I have generally allowed "todt" (as a substantive) to stand wherever it was so printed in the North German hymn-book of 1636. In the version of the Latin hymn "Christe quí lux es et *die*," I have followed the text given by Wackernagel in both editions of his "Das Deutsche Kirchenlied," but I have no doubt that the more usual reading *dies* was also current in Germany, as well as the word *caro* in the third line of the third verse, and that this latter, at least, must have been in the version of the hymn used by the Scottish poet. The word *viel* in the first line of the third stanza of Psalm xiii. is so given by Wackernagel, but in the German Psalm-book of 1537 (a copy of which I have just had an opportunity of examining in the British Museum) it is printed *fiel*, which brings out more fully the correspondence between the Scotch and German versions of that Psalm.

In the Lecture I have indicated my leaning to the opinion that the Wedderburns' collection of hymns and songs, in its most rudimentary form, must have been published before John was obliged to leave his native country in 1546. This is the con-

clusion arrived at by Drs M'Crie and Lorimer, two of the most cautious and
accurate of our ecclesiastical historians; and Lord Hailes and others so far concur
with them as to admit that it must be considered as one, at least, of the collections prohibited by the Canon of the Scottish Ecclesiastical Council of 1549. I do not mean
what is said of the ballads at p. 21 to be more unrestrictedly applied than it is at
pp. 12 and 13; and while I rather incline to look for the "augmentation of sindrie
gude and godlie ballatis not contenit in the first editioun" among the ballads inserted in the first than in the second part of the collection; yet, if any of these
really make reference to later occurrences than I have supposed, they will of course
fall to be included under the same category as those in the first part. In the extract from the books of the king's treasurer, given on page 11, I have followed Dr
M'Crie; but on inspecting the books I find that the last letter of the last word is
followed by a loop and dash, as nearly as possible resembling that which is often
found in writings of that date as a contraction for *is*. It is therefore probable that
the extract should be read "serche James Rollokkis gudis and Maister Johnne
Wedderburnis."

I have to return my best thanks to many kind friends for the aid they have
generously given me in the prosecution of my inquiries, and especially to my friends
David Laing, Esq., of the Signet Library, Edinburgh; W. Wright, Esq., of the O.
MS. Department in the British Museum; and William Bonar, Esq., Sussex Place,
London. After the following sheets were printed, Mr Bonar directed my attention to a
collection of translations and imitations of German hymns, published anonymously
by Messrs Partridge and Oakey, in which it is stated that the Psalms and Songs of
the Wedderburns and Coverdale were *imitations* of those of the German poets, and that
the first stanza of Coverdale's version of Psalm cxxxvii. was a *translation* of Dachstein's German. Had the author of that collection prosecuted his researches, he
would have found that the translation of Dachstein was not confined to the first
stanza of Psalm cxxxvii., but that J. Wedderburn often, and Coverdale almost always,
translates from the German quite as closely as Miss Winkworth or Miss Coxe.
Mr Bonar also called my attention to the fact that in a German edition of Le Long's
Bibliotheca Sacra reference is made to an Enchiridion Psalmorum, printed at Paris
in the year 1581. I found a copy of this in the Bodleian Library at Oxford, and
though the date was subsequent to the death of Wedderburn, and to the publication
of his book, I examined it with some care; but I feel satisfied that it is not the work
referred to in the compendious book of Godly and Spiritual Songs. If I might venture on any more definite conjecture than that given in my Lecture, I would say
that the reference may be to a Latin prose translation of the Psalms, bearing this
title of Enchiridion Psalmorum, which was published as early as 1533, and generally printed in parallel columns with the version of Joannes Campensis. It was
followed in the German Metrical Psalter of 1537, and possibly Wedderburn may
have retained the reference to it from finding it in the German metrical translation
from which he borrowed his Psalms. The German Psalter referred to above contains "ein gespräch des sünders und Christi," which probably supplied Wedderburn with the materials for spiritualizing the old song "Quho is at my windo?
who? who?" while the song to the tune of which that "gespräch" was com-

posed, " Ach Jupiter hättst du gewalt," probably supplied part of the materials for the ballad which he entitles " Ane disswasion from vain lust ;" but the form into which both were cast appears to have been to some extent original. Possibly even the idea of his famous ballad,—" The paip, that pagane full of pryd,"—may have been taken from the German " Nun treiben wir den pabst heraus," but undoubtedly this ballad must have been an imitation and not a translation of the German. An old MS. music book, still preserved in the British Museum, and bearing the date 1530, discloses the fact, that the Roman Catholics in Britain, as well as in Germany, had not disdained to spiritualise popular songs, and had preceded Wedderburn in thus treating the plaintive old ballad, " My love morneth for me." I subjoin it from the copy I made, though, as this was taken hastily and partly in short-hand, I cannot be sure that in every case I have retained the antique spelling :

And I'm unkynd, have not in mynd

Who is my love but God above
And on the rode hys precyous blode
Whom shold I prove so true of love,
That king of blys my love he ys,
The father hys Son from hevyn sent down
The prophecye of Isay
Behold mankynd thy maker most lovyng
What is thy mynd to be so unkynd,
That virgyns child most meke and mylde
Hys fathers wyll for to fulfyl
And soffryd deth, as scrypture sayth,
On good friday, wherefore I say,
Snch payne and smart, as in hys hart
Can no man take nor mournyng make
The cruel Jeus would not refuse
And wyth a dart to perce hys hart,
Now Cryst Jesu my love most treu
I axe thé grace for my trespas
For thy sweet name save me from shame
For Mary's sake to thé me take,

my love that morneth for me for me

that born was of Mary,
he shed to make me fré,
so gentyl and curtes as he,
that mornth so sor for mee,
and born was of a mayd,
fulfyllyd he and sayd,
for thy love come to dye,
syth I so mourne for thé for thé.
alonly for my sake,
he came great payns to take,
that we shuld savyd be
he mournyd sore for me for me.
he suffryd for mankynd,
so mekely for hys frend,
to nayel hym to a tre,
thus mournyd he for me.
have mercy upon me,
that I have done to thé,
and all adversytye,
and mourne no more for me.

From the quotation given above from the title of the compendious book of godly and spiritual songs, there can be no doubt that considerable additions were made to the original collection in the second or subsequent editions. Perhaps the form of some of the pieces contained in the first edition may have been altered, for while Knox tells us that Psalm li., as sung by Wishart, *began* with "Have mercy on me now, good Lord," these words are found in the *second* stanza of the paraphrase as we have it in the later editions of the book. And the very title of the collection appears to have been partially changed ; for while in the edition of 1578 it stands " Ane compendious buik of godlie *Psalmes* and spirituall Sangis," in the edition reprinted by Dalyell, which professed to be " newlie corrected and amended by the first originall copie," it stands, "Ane compendious booke of godly and spirituall songs." It is more difficult to determine whether any of the pieces contained in the original collection were left out in subsequent editions. In a note to page 246, vol. i. of his edition of Knox's History, Mr Laing says that possibly the Wedderburns may have versified more of the Psalms than are contained in this collection. Perhaps it may be regarded as some confirmation of this conjecture that the first line of the Scotch version of Psalm ciii., as given by Knox in the passage referred to, coincides pretty closely with the first line of one of the German paraphrases of the Psalm found in Wackernagel.* And there can be no doubt whatever that translations of some other German hymns, which have not been included in the compendious book, existed in Scotland in the sixteenth century. Besides the version of the Lord's Prayer included in Knox's Psalter, at least two or three of the pieces contained in Wood's MS. book of tunes are undoubtedly derived from this source. One of these, along with a modern English version, will be found inserted at the close of Appendix I. to this Lecture, and another is a version of the "Da pacem, Domine," the German corresponding to which will be found at p. 435 of Wackernagel's "Deutsches Kirchenlied."

A. F. M.

GENEVA, 13th July 1867.

* "My saul praise thow the Lord alwyes," "Mein seel lobt Gott zu aller frist."

CORRIGENDA.

Page 26, line 3, for unsrer read unsren; p. 46, l. 1, after "worthy" insert "gude;" p. 53, l. 26, for rufen read rufen; p. 59, l. 20, for demem read deinem; p. 60, l. 30, for gereuet read gerettet.

LECTURE.

THE SACRED POETRY

OF THE

SCOTTISH REFORMATION.

Your attention has been called by some of my predecessors to foreign lands and manners, to soldiers who fought on foreign fields and gained a name and fame for themselves in the annals of the world. To-night I ask you to give attention to a subject more humble and less exciting, but one connected with our own country and our own corner of it—the story and life work of a family of brothers born and brought up in our own neighbourhood. Their names and services have well nigh perished from the remembrance of their countrymen, but in their day and generation they were a mighty power for good in their native land,—good soldiers of Christ Jesus, and faithful standard-bearers in the Christian army. They fearlessly bore their colours through a long and weary fight, and by their heroic lives and spirit-stirring songs encouraged others to take them up when they had fallen, and to carry on the warfare they had begun, till the banner of the cross was planted triumphantly on the high places of the field, and the glad tidings of a free gospel were once more proclaimed without let or hindrance through the length and breadth of Scotland. My only regret is, that the subject has not fallen into the hands of some one more competent to do full justice to it. but I can

A

honestly say, that the observations regarding it to which I solicit your
attention embody the results of considerable research and reflection, and,
as the subject has grown in interest to myself as I continued to study it,
I am not without hope that even in the shape in which I am able to present it to you, it may prove neither uninteresting nor unimproving, and
that the publication of my address may perhaps direct the attention of
others to the subject, and induce them to aid in the investigation of it.

You are all familiar with the saying of one of our countrymen, "Let
who will make a nation's laws, if I may only make their songs," and
with the fact that, if ever that saying received a signal verification in
history, it was at the time of the Reformation from Popery. The new
and vigorous spiritual life received through the earnest study of the
Word of God, poured itself out in a continuous stream of popular sacred
song, which spread its blessed influence more widely, and made it pene-
trate more deeply. In Italy, as one of the most recent writers on the
subject has in her own thrilling way related it, "from the Gulf of
Genoa to the Adriatic Sea,—in the deep valleys among the purple Ap-
ennines,—in the air-hung villages which gleam among the pine and
chestnut trees on the southern slopes,—and even in queenly Florence,
which a few years later sent the bold friar of San Marco to heaven in a
chariot of fire, simple Italian ballads containing some of the elementary
truths of the gospel were rapidly winning their way among the common
people." "And Savonarola was right and wise, when he trusted the
truths which make wise unto salvation to these airy messengers; it
was not the first time that God had chosen the weak things of the world
to confound the mighty."* "Thirty years later the German churches
were ringing with the hymns of Luther, Eber, Sachs, and Weisse, and
the poetry of the Reformation, wedded to popular music, was treasured
in the households" of the faithful, from the mountains of Switzerland to
the swamps of Holland and the shores of the Baltic, and from the banks
of the Rhine to those of the Vistula and the Danube. The contributions
then furnished laid the foundation of the largest and perhaps the noblest

treasure of Hymnology the Christian Church as yet possesses, and the influence of which continues to be shewn by the translations of its finest hymns into our own and other languages at the present day. "By the middle of the sixteenth century, the reformed hymnology of Denmark had assumed such a position as to call for a history from the pen of Thomässon." Marot's translations of the Psalms and other scriptural songs into French verse were sung with relish even in the dissolute Court of France ; and a Romish cardinal could think of no other way of counteracting their influence but by recommending that an equally spirited translation of the Odes of Horace should be prepared. The only country which may be said to have formed an exception to the general rule, and in which, consequently, the progress of the Reformed doctrines among the common people was far more slow, was England, where there was very little worth mentioning save Sternhold and Hopkins' version of the Psalms of David, and where even that was but little used save among the Puritans. Dr Newman, indeed, used to claim it as a remarkable proof of the caution and wisdom of the English Church, that when she found it necessary to abandon the use of the old Latin hymns, she did not attempt to substitute others in their stead, but was content to be as one beginning the world again, and, like the primitive Church in these respects, poor and ill-furnished.† But she did not think it necessary to act on this principle in drawing up her liturgy, and had the spirit of the grand old Latin hymns really penetrated the English Church and her leaders as thoroughly as it had the German churches and their leaders, there was no reason why the best of these hymns should not have been wedded to the new faith and the popular music in a dress no less attractive, and a form no less quickening, and far more generally influential than the original.

Scotland in this, as in so many other respects, had more in common with the foreign Protestant Churches than with the Church of the sister kingdom. The influence of sacred song in spreading the new faith, and quickening to new and deeper life was no less decided and conspicuous in

---

* M'Crie's Knox, edition 1855, p. 325.   † Preface to his edition of Latin Hymns.

our native land than in continental countries; and after the prayerful
study of the Word of God there was not, during the twenty years of
struggling and suffering which preceded the establishment of the Reformed Church, any instrumentality which contributed so much to keep
alive the faith of the sufferers, to spread their doctrines, and to bring
their opponents and their teaching into the contempt they merited as the
godly and spiritual songs, the tragedies, and ballads of those whom God
had endowed with the gift of poesy, and whose hearts he had touched
with the love of his truth.   It is acknowledged by the apostate Hamilton
that one of the earliest and most effectual means of promoting these ends
was the circulation of certain books in the vernacular dialect, exposing
the vices of the clergy, which were printed in England, and surreptitiously
introduced into the country.*   Probably the metrical address to the Friars
referred to by Row may have been one of these.   Under the year 1539
Calderwood gives us a brief but touching account of " one Kennedy who
had not passed the eighteenth year of his age, a man of good wit and
excelling in Scottish Poesy," who, under a sentence of the Archbishop
of Glasgow, was put to death for his steadfastness in the reformed faith,
and about the same time the Earl of Glencairn " painted forth the hypo-
crisy of the friars in rhyme " in " an epistle directed from the holy hermite
of Larite† to his brethren the Grey Friars."   Most of our historians now
acknowledge the good service done in these early days to the cause of
the Reformation by the tragedies, and other poetical compositions of
Buchanan and Sir David Lindsay,‡ who so fearlessly and mercilessly exposed the follies and vices of the clergy before the nobility and Court of
Scotland.   But there were others who rendered no less essential and
signal service to the cause in these critical times, and who have never yet
received from their country the grateful acknowledgment their services
richly merited.   They laboured not only to pull down but to build up,
and in my humble opinion did more to sustain the spirits of those who
were suffering for the truth and so to ensure the spread and triumph of

* "Immissis in Scotiam libris, atque in vulgus disseminatis, qui sub purioris cujusdam Evangelii
specioso pretextu Ecclesiasticorum virorum vitam et mores odiose traducerent."
† Loretto.   ‡ M'Crie's Knox, p. 25. Row's Hist., p. 6. Cunningham's Church Hist., vol. i., p. 279.

the reformed faith than any of the others referred to. These were the
authors of a collection of sacred songs and ballads mentioned by several
of our writers in the sixteenth and seventeenth centuries under the names
of the "Psalms of Dundee," the "Psalms of Wedderburn," "godly and
spiritual songs," "gude and godly ballates," which seem to have been
published in some shape or other between the years 1542 and 1546, or
several years earlier than the first collected edition of Sir David Lindsay's
poetical works. Being pervaded by deeper earnestness and spirituality,
and setting forth with fond affection and winning simplicity the great
truths of the gospel, they were more completely fitted to meet the felt
wants of the faithful at that trying time, and amidst all conflicts and trials
sustained their faith in God and in His word. They were by no means
deficient in the power of keen irony and cutting satire, and when occasion
seemed to call for it, they dealt with the vices of the clergy quite as unspar-
ingly as the Lyon King at Arms. But they combined with this a more
intense and unvarying moral purpose, and at times a deep and yearning
tenderness which added to their power both of shaming from sin and
stimulating to all that was holy and good and true, tending to imbue the
mind with a purer faith and higher life, and to encourage to Christian
steadfastness and boldness even at the risk of imprisonment and death.
Probably the range of their circulation was rather among the middle than
among the higher classes of our countrymen, and especially among the substantial burghers of our trading communities, but among these classes their
influence was conspicuous and acknowledged, and along with the spirit-
stirring sermons of their great preachers, contributed to make them,—
what they long continued to be,—the chief strength of the Reformed
Church. Nor did the range of their circulation diminish after the triumph of the reformed faith had been secured, but for considerably more
than half a century they continued to be treasured in the hearts of the
people and sung in their households.* They soothed the chafed spirit
of Wishart on the night of his betrayal, nourished the early piety of the
younger Melville when at school in Montrose, and comforted the hearts

* An edition of the "gude and godly ballads" was printed as late as 1621

of mourners in that district as they performed the last office of kind
ness to departed friends.

The story of their authors may be soon told. For though much has
been done of late years to vindicate the character of Knox, as one of the
truest patriots his country ever had, and to set in clearer light the brief
but sad story of Patrick Hamilton and George Wishart, and to remove
the haze that had gathered round the form of Alesius, or Alan, the
young exile, who, by his tracts and treatises, aroused among his countrymen a general and irrepressible longing to be allowed to read the word of
God in their own tongue; yet I regret to say that the history of the
authors of this collection of sacred songs remains still to be investigated
and recorded; and that, with all the time I have given to the subject, I
have been able to glean but a very few facts in addition to those few
which Calderwood long ago collected respecting them.

The teaching of that amiable and accomplished youth, Patrick
Hamilton, confirmed by his martyr death, and by the sad end of his be-
trayer, appears to have made a deep and lasting impression on the minds
of the less prejudiced graduates of the University, and the less dissolute
monks in the monasteries of St Andrews. Mr Gavin Logie, the prin-
cipal regent in the newly founded College of St Leonards, all but openly
endeavoured to indoctrinate his pupils with the new faith, so that, " he
has drunk of St Leonard's well," became a proverbial expression to indi-
cate of any one that he had imbibed the principles and doctrines of the
Reformers. Among those who, as associates or pupils, profited by his
instructions, and became warmly attached to his person, were Alexander
Alan or Alesius, already mentioned, and John Fyff or Fidelis, both of
whom, after suffering imprisonment for their opinions, sought safety in
flight. After a time, they found their way to Wittenberg, renewed
their studies there, and were ultimately advanced to be Professors of
Divinity at Leipsic and Frankfort on the Oder. A third, named Henry
Forrest, was subjected to a still more cruel imprisonment in the Sea tower
of the Castle of St Andrews, and only came forth from prison to win the
martyr's crown. Logie himself escaped to England about the year 1533,
and came no more into public notice.

Among the knot of talented and earnest young men who are said to
have gathered around Logie between the years 1516 and 1533, there
were three brothers, bearing the names of James, John, and Robert
Wedderburn, sons of James Wedderburn, merchant at the West Kirk Style
of Dundee. Their father was probably of the old Forfarshire family of
Wedderburn, and was evidently a man of considerable wealth and standing,
as his son John is entered in the University register as *dives*. They
are said by Calderwood to have gained their first knowledge of the truth
from their regent Logie; but from the University register it appears that
one of them, at least for a time, was a student in the "Predagogium," or,
as it was afterwards called, St Mary's College, and was in residence the
very year that Patrick Hamilton was incorporated into the University,
and was permitted to teach in it. There is no reason to suppose, however, that at that time they acquired anything more than a general liking
for the new faith, and the men who taught it; and, in fact, Calderwood
tells us that it was only after their return to their native place, and in
consequence of the instructions of Friar Hewat, a Dominican monk in
the monastery of that order in Dundee, that they were led on to deeper
and clearer views of the truth. At length they became open professors
and steadfast confessors of the new faith; and, having drunk of the
Pierian spring as well as of St Leonard's well, they used in defence and
propagation of their faith the invaluable gift of poesy with which God
had endowed them. The eldest brother, James, studied at St Andrews,
but does not appear to have proceeded to the degree either of Bachelor
or Master of Arts. His name appears in the list of those incorporated
into the University in the year 1516; and Calderwood adds that he
studied in St Leonard's College, under Mr Gavin Logie, and was reason-
ably well instructed in philosophy and humanity. After leaving College
he went for some time to France, perhaps to acquire a more thorough knowledge of his profession; and after his return to his native place he was
fully instructed in the knowledge of the truth by Hewat, who had been
sup-prior of the Dominican monastery at Perth, and who probably held
some similar office in the house of that order in Dundee. He composed
several tragedies and comedies in his native tongue, in which, after the

example of Buchanan and Lindsay, he exposed the corruption of the clergy, and the abuses of the Church. One of these compositions was a mystery, or sacred tragedy, on the beheading of John the Baptist, which, Calderwood informs us, was acted at the West Port of Dundee ; and another was a comedy compiled out of the history of Dionysius the tyrant, which the same historian tells us was acted in the playfield of the said burgh. In both of these plays he lashed the vices of the popish ecclesiastics, and especially, we may suppose, of that clever, cruel, dissolute tyrant, Cardinal Beaton, who cherished such lasting and bitter enmity to him and his brothers. No fragment of either has come down to us, but no doubt we have a fair exhibition of their spirit and sentiments, if not also of their contents,* in some of the pieces in the collection to be more particularly noticed by and bye, and especially in one which seems to me to have been meant to apply to the Cardinal in the height of his prosperity :

"The Bishop of Hely† brake his neck,
    Disherist of his benefice,
Cause hee the priests wald not correct,
    Corruptand Godis sacrifice.
Sin our Hely in his office,
    Is like in prevarication,
He sall receive sic like justice,
    Make hee not reformation."

            .   .   .

"For your abuse may be ane brother
    To Pharo's als like in similitude
As ever ane egge was like ane other,
    Of Godis word baith destitude ;
And [the] great God in sanctitude,
    Quhais power has nought tane ane
        end,
Sall send with that same fortitude,
    Sic like on you, except ye mend.

" All the examples of the law
    Are written with greit diligence,
For ourselves that we stand awe
    Of Godis hie magnificence.
Of this we have experience
    Of diverse nations round about,
For Ingles prelates, Dutch and Dence,
    For their abuse are rutted out.

" Reforme in time, leave your tyrannie ;
    First mend your life, syne learn to
        preich,
Thocht vagrant friars fain wald lie,
    The truth will furth, and will not leich,
For everie man does other teich,
    And countis nocht your crueltie ;
Except ye mend, I will not fleich,
    Yee sall end all mischevouslie."‡

---

* Some of the German mysteries or sacred plays at least contain songs of similar import.
† I suppose of course that the High Priest Eli is meant.
‡ Compendious book of godly and spiritual songs : Dalzell's edition, pp. 169. 170.

James Wedderburn, Calderwood tells us, composed another play in which he counterfeited the conjuring of a ghaist, which feat had in sober earnest been attempted at Kinghorn by Friar Laing, the king's confessor : but as that piece of folly had cost the friar his place, so the burlesquing of it brought on James Wedderburn a life-long exile from his native land. "He was delated to the king, and letters of caption were directed against him in the year 1540, but he escaped secretly to France, and established himself as a merchant at Rouen or Dieppe, where he lived in prosperity and died in peace.* The youngest brother, Robert, was incorporated into St. Leonard's College in the year 1526, and took both his Bachelor's and Master's degree in the year 1530. From his name appearing first in the books on both occasions, though it was not entitled to come first in alphabetical order, we may infer that he was a distinguished student, and Calderwood informs us that he excelled his brother both in classical learning and in scriptural knowledge. He was early admitted to priest's orders, and ultimately succeeded his mother's brother as Vicar of Dundee, in which office we cannot doubt that he would water the seed which Wishart and Hewat had sown, and by his teaching and living contribute to make Dundee what it so early became—one of the strongholds of the Reformation. But he also, at least during the life of Cardinal Beaton, had to seek safety in flight to a foreign land, and even after his return he resided a great deal with the laird of Calder. He is said to have superintended the editing of the godly and spiritual songs after his brother's death, and to have taken great pains to provide for the various metres pleasing and appropriate tunes.† The second brother, John, is said by Calderwood to have also studied under Gavin Logy in St. Leonard's College, and it is just possible that he may have done so for a year, but in the University books he appears among those incorporated into what was then the "pædagogium," and afterwards became St. Mary's College, and that in the very year when Buchanan also was there. In the following year he appears among the Determinants from the pædagogium. He took his Bachelor's degree in 1526 and his Master's in 1528. It will thus be seen that he was at St. Andrews at the very time that Patrick Hamilton was

* Calderwood's History, Wodrow Society's Edition, vol. 1, p. 142.   † Ibid. p. 143.

B

there, and may have had the opportunity of listening to his lessons as well
as to those of Logy, and perhaps may have had his love of sacred song
quickened by attending on the instructions which Hamilton is said to have
given in sacred music. It is not impossible he may have witnessed that
sad scene which was exhibited at the gates of St. Salvador's College on
the last day of February 1528, when the amiable and youthful martyr
sealed his testimony with his blood, and that it was the deep impression
then made on his spirit which led him to indite such verses as the following :—

"They brunt and heryit Christen men,   "Heretiks they did us call
    And flemit them full sair,   Cursand us night and day,
    They said they did but erre   The truth durst no man say ;
That spake of the commandments ten,   Trew preachers were forbidden all
    Or read the word of Jesus Christ.   To shaw the word of Jesus Christ."

But whatever impression may have been made on John Wedderburn's
spirit by what he saw and heard in St. Andrews, it was only, Calderwood tells us, after his return to his native place, and being favoured
with the instructions and counsels of Friar Hewat, that he came to the
full knowledge of the truth. He had been persuaded by his friends to
enter into priest's orders, and for a time he, as well as his younger brother,
acted as a priest in Dundee ; but when he learned the way of God more
perfectly he made open profession of his faith, and in consequence of this,
or not improbably in consequence of some overt act in that field of literature in which he afterwards became famous, he was summoned before
the authorities on the charge of heresy. Whether he appeared, and was
convicted after trial, and then succeeded in effecting his escape, or whether
he fled before his trial, and was condemned in his absence, cannot be
quite definitely ascertained. The latter supposition seems more accordant
with the statement of Calderwood, but the former appears to me to be
more countenanced by the entries from the books of the king's treasurer,
which Dr. M'Crie has given in one of the notes to his ' Life of Knox."
It is expressly said of a number of the persons mentioned in these entries
that they were fugitive and condemned ; but of Maister Johnne Wedderburn it is simply said that he had been convicted of certain charges of

heresy,* and his goods, in consequence, escheated to his Majesty's use, who was graciously pleased for a small composition to make a gift of them to his brother Henry. From another entry in the same books we learn that in March 1538-39 a "pursevant" was directed to pass to Dundee and "serche James Rollokkis gudis, *and Maister Johnne Wedderburn.*" This entry no doubt furnishes the reason of the former one, though, as being part of his discharge, it is inserted in the Treasurer's books after it; and in connection with the punishment inflicted it renders it very probable that the crime of which Rollok and Wedderburn were convicted was that of having in their possession prohibited books. From the other entry being included in the books for that year, it is more likely that Wedderburn's conviction and flight took place in 1539 than in 1540. There is no doubt as to the fact that he succeeded in effecting his escape from his persecutors, and, after a short time, in finding his way to Wittenberg—that school of the prophets which was then attracting to it so many noble, generous, and earnest young spirits. There he joined his countrymen Alesius, Fyff, and M'Alpine, exiles from their native land for the same cause as himself, and with them and many talented refugees from other lands, drunk in the truth as it flowed, warm and fresh, from the heart and lips of Luther and Melanchthon—striving to mould his character by the high model these good and great men set before him, and to refresh his spirit by Christian intercourse with them, and by deep draughts from the precious stream then being poured forth from the long sealed fountain of sacred song. The influence of these happy years on Wedderburn seems to have been specially marked, and to the opportunities he then enjoyed we must ascribe the firm and practical hold he got and retained, of the great principles of the evangelical theology, which he iterates and reiterates in his poetical compositions with singular constancy and prominence. So marked is this peculiarity, that even when his poems are translations, he often departs from the original to set forth more clearly and simply the way of salvation through the atoning death

* Perhaps the following lines may have some reference to his own case as well as to that of others—

" At midnight mirk they will us take
And into prison will us fling,
There mon we be till we forsake
The name of God quhilk is our King.

Then faggots man we burn or bear,
Or to the deid they will us bring.
It does them gude to do us dear,
And to confusion us down thring."

and justifying righteousness of the Lord Jesus Christ, so that even the
most heedless who might peruse his hymns and ballads might be left
without excuse.if they continued to neglect the great salvation.   After
the death of King James V. in December 1542, when the Cardinal was
under restraint, and the supreme power of the state had fallen into the
hands of one who professed to be friendly to the cause of the Reformation, and who had just let pass through Parliament an act permitting the
Scriptures to be read in the English or the Scottish tongue, John Wedderburn returned to his native land with his harp strung and tuned to
sing in rude Scottish verse those noble songs which had touched his own
heart in exile, as they had touched and moved the hearts of the German
people, and amidst all their wanderings have continued to do so even to
the present day.   It is principally to John Wedderburn, the second of
this noble band of brothers, that we owe, as is generally supposed, the
compendious book of godly and spiritual songs, psalms, and ballads, the
wide circulation and great influence of which, in those years of peril and
persecution which preceded the ultimate triumph of the Reformed cause,
are acknowledged by Row, and some others of our ecclesiastical historians.[*]
It is not improbable that it was begun while he was abroad and using
those songs of the German Church, to which we shall find many of his
own bear a close resemblance—perhaps at the suggestion of the same
wise and thoughtful counsellor who had encouraged Alesius to contend
so vigorously for the free circulation of the word of God in Scotland—
the good and gentle Melanchthon, to whom, through his two pupils, our
native country owes a debt of gratitude which its historians have hitherto
been slow to acknowledge.   What part of the collection first appeared,
and when and where it was published, cannot now be ascertained, as the
earliest edition of which a copy has been discovered—that of 1578, makes
distinct reference to an earlier and less complete one.   The probability is
that some of the ballads may have been printed separately, and sold
through the country soon after the author's return from his first exile—
perhaps two or three of them which make reference to the disagreement
between Henry VIII. and James V., or to the breach of the treaty for
the marriage of the Prince Edward of England with the Princess Mary

* Row's History. Wodrow Society's edition, p. 6.   See also M'Crie, Lorimer, and Cunningham.

of Scotland, and the wars between the two countries, and the destruction of religious houses which ensued*—those which allude to the refusal of the Popish Prelates generally to attend a General Council for the Reformation of the Church, and that already quoted and seemingly addressed to the Head of the Popish Clergy in Scotland. Had this not been written and come abroad while "my lord Cardinal" was still in the height of his power, doubtless his sad fate would have been adduced as a more impressive warning to his successor than the rooting out of "English prelates, Dence, or Dutch." Then, as Dr M'Crie has observed,† some of the Psalms in the collection (and probably, therefore, the collection itself in its most rudimentary form) must have been published before the death of Wishart, as it is expressly stated by Knox, that on the night in which he was apprehended, the martyr had sung part of the Fifty-First Psalm in Scottish metre, and the two lines which Knox gives coincide with no other known version of that Psalm than the long paraphrase of it found among these "godly and spirituall sangs." Moreover, as we do not hear of any overt act by which he could have so exasperated the clergy that he should have been obliged again to flee from his native country in 1546, and to remain in exile even after the cardinal's death and the return of his brother, it is only natural to conclude that it must have been owing to the publication of his songs and ballads. This conclusion is confirmed by some lines in Johnstoue's poem in his praise, which at once plainly point to his poems as the cause of the hard usage he received, and attest what Row says respecting their influence in the years of depression and persecution immediately preceding the final struggle and triumph of the Reformers. There can be little doubt that Wedderburn's book was the chief of those aimed at in the canon made at the Council of the Scottish Clergy in 1549, wherein it was enjoined that search should be made in the several dioceses for those who retain in their possession any books of rhymes or ballads, containing either scandalous charges against the clergy and their constitutions, or any heresy;—that the books, where found, should be confiscated and burnt, and that the sale,

printing, and reading of them should be prohibited under the severe
penalties contained in the Acts of Parliament.*   The Acts of Parliament
previous to this date had not expressly named metrical productions as
distinct from other heretical books, but the Acts of subsequent Parlia-
ments do ; and yet notwithstanding this and the canons of subsequent
ecclesiastical councils, the "compendious booke of godly and spirituall
sangs" continued without any direct ecclesiastical sanction to maintain
its place in the hearts and households of the Scottish people, and in the
course of the succeeding half century passed through several editions.   In
the early part of the seventeenth century it appears gradually to have
fallen into disuse ; even Calderwood seems to have had but an indistinct
notion of its origin, and our church historians ever since, if they have
condescended to notice it at all, have contented themselves with giving a
very meagre account of its contents and historical relations.   The author
is supposed to have lived chiefly in England during the ten long years of
his second exile, and to have died there in 1556.   The lines of John-
stone in his praise,† already referred to, are, perhaps, the most emphatic
testimony to his worth and work which has come down to us from the
time when he was still well-remembered, and settle beyond question the
fact that it was to him our fathers chiefly owed those songs which they
so greatly valued.   Nearly seventy years have now elapsed since these
godly and spiritual songs were last reprinted, and that in a very incorrect

---

* Robertson's Statuta Ecclesiæ Scoticanæ, vol. ii., p. 120.   The learned editor, whose early removal
has occasioned unfeigned sorrow to all who knew him, says (vol. i., p. clxii.), that the framers of this
canon, no doubt, had Lindsay's satires in view.   I have not been able to find any evidence that these had
been published at so early a date ; and a few years later, when they are believed to have been published,
the Act of Parliament makes more express mention of the class of works to which they belong.   "The
new Dialoge callit Pasculluis," which he tells us (vol. ii., p. 294) was prohibited by the Privy Council in
1543, bears a suspicious resemblance in its title to "ein neuer Pasquillus," published in Germany in 1541.

† "Non meriti est nostri, meritas tibi dicere grates,
     Aut paria, aut aliquâ parte referre vicem.
   Quæ meruisse alii vellent, nec posse mereri est :
   Hæc velle, hæc posse, hæc te meruisse tuum est.
   Sic facis atque canis sacra : sic agis omnia, nil ut
   Sanctius, et nusquam purior ulla fides.
   Hinc nullum magis invisum caput hostibus: hinc et
   Nemo unquam meruit charior esse bonis.
   Grandius hoc meritum, nil te meruisse fateris.
   Humani meritis nec superesse locum."

or at least uncorrected form.* The editor, as will be shown by and bye, did not fully understand some of the statements of Calderwood, and he has added nothing really important to them. Mr David Laing, to whom we owe so many valuable reprints of the works of our Reformers, is at present engaged in preparing a new edition of these songs from the earliest edition yet discovered, which will be far more carefully executed, and will be accompanied with a historical introduction, which, I doubt not, will add much to our information, and, I trust, will direct more general attention to this favourite book of our reforming fathers.

My thoughts were first specially turned to the book in the spring of last year, by finding several pieces from it inserted at length in a very interesting volume published by the Rev. Dr Bonar of Kelso, and entitled "Catechisms of the Reformation." I do not know whether it was that the spirit of contradiction had been aroused in me by what appeared to me to be needless depreciation of Luther's Catechism, and rather unmeasured laudation of Wedderburn's, as so far in advance of Luther's; or whether my zest after such correspondences had been unduly quickened by some other discoveries I seemed to have fallen on, but so it was, that when I turned from Dr Bonar's preface to the extracts he gave from the first part of Wedderburn's book, I was at once startled by the fact that the commandments appeared to be given in the Lutheran form, and that if the doctrine taught in the hymns on baptism and the Lord's Supper was not narrowly and distinctively Lutheran, it was not in any respect markedly at variance with that which Luther taught. Then, on careful examination, the measure and ring of the metrical version of the Creed reminded me unmistakeably of Luther's famous hymn on the same subject; and the last hymn extracted from the collection by Dr Bonar at once recalled to my mind a hymn of the same era, which is still sung at funerals in Germany. By a reference to my German hymn books, I soon satisfied myself that three of the nine poetical pieces extracted by Dr Bonar from the Scotch collection were pretty close translations from the German; and other three, though apparently far less close, yet, by

---

* No attempt was made to correct nor even to point out such evident blunders as "*dil*" for "*dei*," "*principio*" for "*præcepio*," "*A per C*" for "*A per se*," "*crusifge*" for "*crucifig*;" nor even the manifest errors in the numbering of the Psalms, as xxiv. for xiv., lxxii. for cxiii., &c.

the similarity of their metre, or by occasional verbal coincidences, gave unmistakeable evidence of their origin. The metrical graces, and the other three longer pieces extracted by Dr Bonar from Wedderburn's collection I did not, with the materials then at my command, succeed in tracing to a foreign source, and I laid the matter aside for a time, till I should have more leisure, and farther means of prosecuting my inquiries. When in Edinburgh in June last, I brought the subject and my conjecture respecting it under the notice of an honoured friend, to whose more extensive knowledge, and more matured judgment in all questions connected with the history and literature of the Reformation I am accustomed to defer, but he did not appear to have had his attention specially called to it before, or to have heard of such very close resemblance being traced between these Scottish and the old German hymns, and could only advise me to proceed with caution, as possibly the resemblances might be satisfactorily accounted for by the derivation both of the Scotch and German hymns from the Latin. I therefore asked a friend who was a better German scholar than myself to take Dalyell's reprint of the ' godlie and spiritual sangs, and to compare its contents with those of his German hymn books, and to let me know the result. But his hymnbooks, like my own, contained only a small number of the older German hymns, and so he did not succeed in tracing any correspondence save in the case of three more than had at first struck me. Thus the matter rested till the end of autumn, when it occurred to me that the subject was one which, in the infirm state of my health, I might prosecute with interest, and yet without exhaustive mental labour. Accordingly I provided myself with farther materials for carrying on the inquiry and particularly with an old German hymn-book, with Wackernagel's " Deutsches Kirchenlied, and several of his valuable works on the Bibliography of German Hymns. A repeated and careful examination of these several books has enabled me to trace fully one-half of the compositions contained in the first part of the " compendious booke of godly and spiritual sangs" to a German origin, several of them, though executed with good taste and poetic spirit, being rendered almost line for line from the German, others being far more free as well as spirited translations, and some giving indication of their origin only by a general similarity, by occasional verbal coincidences, and the adoption of the same metre and refrain as the corresponding German Hymn. On closer examination of the " compendious booke " itself, also, I found it contained a notice which, beyond all question, must settle the character of its second part, and which it is very strange should have hitherto attracted so little special attention. It runs as follows, " Heir ends the spirituall sangs and begins the Psalms of David with other new and pleasant ballates *translat.d out of* Enchiridion Psalmorum to be sung." From this notice it is plain that whatever may be the case with the hymns which precede it, those which follow are confessedly to be regarded as mostly translations from some previously existing work, and yet this is the very fact of which not even one of those who have directed attention to the book seem to have had the least idea. But what is "Enchiridion Psalmorum?" The friend to whom I communicated my first conjectures has even with his great knowledge of the books and history of the time as yet been unable fully to determine this question, and it is hardly to be expected I should be able to do so. Yet I shall try to cut if not to loose this Gordian knot. A careful examination of the Bibliographical treatises of Wackernagel discloses the fact that between the years 1524 and 1570, a large number of editions of Hymn-books, bearing the general name of Enchiridion or Handbüchlein, issued from the German press, which generally contained in their first part some such collection of "Geistliche Gesänge " or "spiritual sangs," as is given in the first part of Wedderburn's compendious book, and in their second, " Psalmen und Lieder " which I suppose may without much forcing be rendered " Psalmes and Ballates." Very probably it is to one of these Enchiridia that reference is made in the notice given above.* The first of them was published at Erfurt in 1524, and it is in another of them, apparently published at the same place in 1528, that the version of the second Psalm—pretty freely rendered by Wedderburn —is supposed to have been first published. It is rather, however, to one or other of the Strassburg Hymn-books, that I am disposed to trace

* It would be rash in me to assert the " Enchiridion " cannot *possibly* have been the name of a Latin collection, but if so it must have been a collection of translations from the German like those of Helmbold, Fabricius, Ammonius, &c. Wedderburn's translation of Psalm is is more like to the German than to their Latin versions of it, or even to that of Mourett.

this second part of Wedderburn's book, in so far as it may be a translation,
and these, in so far as their versions of the Psalms are concerned, are
derived chiefly from a Swiss Hymn-book published at Zurich in the year
1536, which has now so completely disappeared that even Wackernagel
has not been able to ascertain its exact title.

After a short prologue* the "compendious booke" commences with
what has been very properly denominated the catechism as containing
the elementary instruction which was intended to be specially impressed
on the minds of the young and ignorant. The text or prose version of
the Ten Commandments, the Creed, the Lord's Prayer, the institution
of baptism, and of the Lord's Supper is first given,—and this not from any
English version of the Scriptures with which I am acquainted, but rather
from Luther's German, though there is one peculiar rendering that is hardly
accounted for even thus. After these prose extracts come five metrical
hymns, three of which are pretty close yet spirited translations of Luther's
hymns on the Creed, on Baptism, and the Lord's Supper. The stanza
and refrain of the metrical version of the Ten Commandments are the
same as Luther's, and the first and second commandments are joined to-
gether as in Luther's hymn, but the explanations of the individual commandments are not very similar,† and the commencement of the song
more closely resembles another German metrical version of the commandments, of which Wackernagel has given only the first line. The
metrical version of the Lord's Prayer, though composed in the same six-
lined stanza as Luther's and several of the German versions, does not
closely resemble any of them which I have yet seen;‡ but it is rather
remarkable, that while the versions of the Ten Commandments and of
the Creed appended to Knox's Psalter are taken from the French, the
version of the Lord's Prayer which follows them is a singularly faithful
yet spirited translation of Luther's hymn, not unworthy to stand side by
side with any of the more recent English translations of it.§ To

---

* The edition of 1578, has, like many of the German Hymn-books, a calendar.

† They bear a somewhat closer resemblance to those of Weisse, whose hymn has the same form of
stanza and the same refrain as Luther's.

‡ At least ten are given in Wackernagel's "Das Deutsche Kirchenlied."   § See Appendix II.

these five hymns in Wedderburn's book succeed various metrical graces, to be said before and after meat, some of which may be found in old German hymn-books, and the longest of which is taken almost line for line from one which still holds its place in some modern German collections. The spiritual songs proper of the Scotch book begin with two confessions of sin, a song of the contest between the flesh and the spirit, and a song of the cross and the fruit thereof, the last three of which are close versions of German hymns given in Wackernagel's collection, and the first bears considerable resemblance to one of those given in Hommel's Supplement to Wackernagel's work. Then follow rather lengthy paraphrases of the parables of the prodigal son and of the rich man and Lazarus, which are probably abridgements of German paraphrases of these passages of Scripture which we know from Wackernagel were in circulation as early as the year 1536. To these succeed a metrical version of the history of our Lord's passion—a pretty close rendering of an old German hymn still to be found in some of the modern collections, and "ane sang of the Evangel," which is a less close but more spirited translation of the first hymn Luther composed. After these come four hymns on the incarnation and birth of Christ, three of which still hold their places in the German hymn-books, and are among the finest of the many fine hymns on this subject which the German Church possesses. The Scottish version of the first of them is quite worthy, in respect of pathos and poetic merit, to take its place side by side with either of the two beautiful versions of it in English which have been published in our own day. The second, third, and fourth are versions of hymns that came to the German reformed Church through the Latin ; but though they are all executed with considerable spirit, the resemblance of all of them to the German version in its variations from the Latin is too marked to leave any doubt that they, like so many of the others, are taken directly from the German. The second contains one stanza which is not found in the common German copies. The fourth contains some typographical errors, which a reference to the German enables us to correct. The third is one of the wildest lilts the mediæval Church possessed, and its odd mixture of Scotch and Latin is a faithful reproduction of the mixture of German and Latin which was the favourite form of this hymn in the early part of the sixteenth century. After these hymns on the birth of Christ come a song of thanksgiving to God for once more spreading among men the knowledge of His word—a pretty close rendering of a German hymn attributed to Speratus, and a metrical version of the Song of Simeon, which is in the same stanza as that of Luther, and is probably a free rendering of it or of some of the other German versions modelled on it. These are succeeded by a brief hymn entitled " ane sang of the resurrection," which is the only one in the first part of the book of which I think myself entitled to say with any confidence, that it appears to be more immediately derived from the Latin than the German. At least it more closely resembles a Latin hymn found in several of the German hymn-books than any of the German versions of it I have yet seen. The first part of the collection then winds up with a number of miscellaneous pieces, several of which have no distinct titles, and are of inferior merit to those which precede. I have as yet succeeded in tracing only three or four of these to German sources, but I am not without hope that a more careful search will lead to the identification of at least as many more of the hymns on the birth of Christ with Latin or German originals.

The second part of the collection, as I have already mentioned, is, in the main, avowedly a translation from some previously existing work. It consists partly of a selection of Psalms (2, 12,* 13, 15, 23, 33, 37, 64, 73, 83, 91, 114, 115, 124, 130, 137, 145, 79, 51, 128, 67, 31,) several hymns not inferior in pathos and beauty to any of those in the first part, and some of which I have ascertained to be also translations from the German, several adaptations of profane or secular songs to religious subjects, and a considerable number of ballads exposing in a very pithy and earnest manner, the corruptions of the clergy and the abuses of the Church, yet to a great extent free from the coarseness which characterizes some of the ablest pieces of Sir David Lindsay, and from the fierce re-

* This is given as the eleventh, and generally the numbers of the Vulgate are followed, and the initial word of the Latin are prefixed. Psalms 114 and 115 are given as one Psalm and numbered 113. Psalm lxxix. is numbered lxxvii., and singularly enough this mistake also occurs in the Strassburg Hymn-book of 1547 if not in that of 1545. Of course the number in the Vulgate is lxxviii.

vengeful spirit which several of the English poets of the same era exhibit,
and which the cruelties inflicted on the author and his friends would to
some extent have palliated. The idea of some, even of these ballads, may
have been suggested by the German Volkslieder on the same subjects, but
the most of them no doubt are original, and it is not at all unlikely that
some of them at first made their appearance separately, and had a partial
circulation before obtaining a place in the compendious booke of godly
and spiritual songs, and as external evidence seems to favour the conclusion that some part of the book must have been printed before 1546, so,
as has been already hinted, the internal evidence seems to shew that
these ballads must have been written and printed *at latest* before their
author left Scotland in that year.

To bring out the full extent of the resemblance between these early
Scotch and the German hymns, I shall in an appendix exhibit in parallel
columns the text of several of them in both languages, and for the sake
of those who do not know German, I subjoin here in parallel columns
the Scotch versions of three or four of them, and one or other of the
English versions of the same German hymns executed in our own day.

The first I give is that which at once struck me on reading Dr Bonar's
book, the metrical version of the creed, and alongside of this I place the
admirable version of Luther's hymn by Miss Winkworth. It will be
observed at once that the stanza of Miss Winkworth is shorter by a line
than Wedderburn's. The explanation of this is that she has cast into her
ninth line what forms two short lines in the original, and in singing needs
to be repeated in whole or in part ; while Wedderburn, as he often does,
has lengthened both lines that he might give a separate syllable to each
note of the music.

CREID.	CREED.
We trow in God allanerly,	We all believe in one true God,
Full of micht and majesty,	Maker of the earth and heaven ;
Maker of hevin and eird sa braid,	The Father, who to us in love,
Quhilk hes him selfe our Father maid.	Hath the claim of children given.
And we his sonnes ar in deid,	He in soul and body feeds us,
He will us keip in all our neid,	All we want His hand provides u :

Baith saule and body to defend,
That no mischance sall us offend ;
He takis cure baith day and nicht,
To saue us throw his godly micht,
From Sathan's subtilty and slicht.

We trow in Jesus Christ his Sone,
God lyke in gloir, our Lord allone,
Quhilk, for his mercy and his grace,
Wald man be born to mak our peace,
Of Marie mother Virgin chast,
Consevit be the Haly Ghaist,
And for our saik on croce did die,
Fra sin and hell to mak us free,
And rais from deith throw his godheid,
Our Mediatour and our remeid,
Sall cum to judge baith quick and deid.

We trow in God the Haly Spreit,
In all destres our comfort sweit :
We trow the Kirk Catholick be,
And faithfull Christin companie,
Throw all the warld with ane accord :*
Remission of our sin we trow,
And this same flesche that levis now,
Sall stand up at the latter day,
And bruke eternall life for ay.

Thro' all snares and perils leads us,
    Watches that no harm betides us ;
He cares for us by day and night,
All things are governed by His might.

And we believe in Jesus Christ,
    His only Son, our Lord, possessing
An equal Godhead, throne and might,
    Through whom descends the Father's
        blessing ;
Conceivèd of the Holy Spirit,
    Born of Mary, virgin mother ;
That lost man might life inherit,
    Made true man, our elder Brother
Was crucified for sinful men,
    And raised by God to life again.

And we confess the Holy Ghost,
    Who from Son and Father floweth,
The Comforter of fearful hearts,
    Who all precious gifts bestoweth ;
In whom all the Church hath union,
Who maintains the saint's communion;
    We believe our sins forgiven,
    And that life with God in heaven,
When we are raised again, shall be
Our portion in eternity.

The next I give has the quaint title, " Ane sang of the birth of Christ with the tune of Baw lulalaw." It is Luther's hymn, which he composed for his little boy Hans, and which is still shouted from the steeple in some German cities early on Christmas morning. Alongside of the Scotch version I give the English one made by Miss Winkworth in our own day. A version still closer to the original has still more recently been furnished in the " Sunday Magazine."

* A line which should have rhymed with this has possibly dropped out.

ANE SANG OF THE BIRTH OF CHRIST.

With the tune of Baw lulalaw.

I come from hevin to tell
The best nowellis that ever be fell,
To you thir tythinges trew I bring,
And I will of them say and sing.

This day to you is borne ane childe,
Of Marie meike, and Virgine mylde;
That blissit bairne, bening and kynde,
Sall you rejoice baith heart and mynd.

It is the Lord Christ, God and man,
Hee will doe for you quhat hee can;
Himselfe your Sauiour hee will bee,
Fra sinne and hell to make yow free.

He is our richt saluation,
From everlasting damnation,
That ye may ring in gloir and blis,
For ever mair in hevin with his.

Ye sall him find but marke or wring,
Full sempill in ane crib lying;
So lyis hee quhilk yow hes wrocht,
And all this warld made of nocht.

Let us rejoyce and be blyth,
And with the hyrdes goe full swyth,
And see quhat God of his grace hes don
Throw Christ to bring us to his throne.

My saull and lyfe, stand up and see
Quha lyes in ane crib of tree;
Quhat babe is that so gude and faire?
It is Christ, God's Sonne and Aire.

CHRISTMAS HYMN.

Vom himmel hoch da komm ich her.

From heaven above to earth I come
To bear good news to every home;
Glad tidings of great joy I bring,
Whereof I now will say and sing.

To you this night is born a child
Of Mary, chosen mother mild;
This little child, of lowly birth,
Shall be the joy of all your earth.

'Tis Christ, our God, who far on high
Hath heard your sad and bitter cry;
Himself will your salvation be,
Himself from sin will make you free.

He brings those blessings, long ago
Prepared by God for all below;
Henceforth his kingdom open stands
To you, as to the angel bands.

These are the tokens ye shall mark,
The swaddling clothes and manger dark;
There shall you find the young child laid,
By whom the heavens and earth were
    made.

Now let us all with gladsome cheer
Follow the shepherds, and draw near
To see this wondrous gift of God,
Who hath His only Son bestowed.

Give heed, my heart, lift up thine eyes!
Who is it in yon manger lies?
Who is this child, so young and fair?
The blessed Christ-child lieth there.

Welcome now, gracious God of mycht,
To sinners vyle, pure and unricht;
Thou come to saue us from distresse,
How can wee thank thy gentilnesse?

O God that made all creature,
How art thow becum so pure,
That on the hay and stray will lye,
Amang the asses, oxin and kye?

And were the warld ten tymes so wide,
Cled ouer with gold and stanes of pride,
Unworthy yit it were to thee,
Under thy feit ane stule to bee.

The sylke and sandell, thee to eis,
Are hay and sempill sweiling clais,
Quhairin thow gloiris, greitest king,
As thou in hevin were in thy ring.

Thow tuke like paines temporall,
To make me riche perpetuall;
For all this warldis welth and gude,
Can nothing richt thy celsitude.

O my deir hert, young Jesus sweit,
Prepare thy creddill in my spreit,
And I sall rocke thee in my hert,
And never mair from thee depart.

But I sall praise thee evermoir,
With sangs sweit unto thy gloir;
The knees of my hert sall I bow,
And sing that richt Balulalow.

Gloir bee to God eternally,
Quhilk gaif his only Sonne for me,

Welcome to earth, Thou noble guest,
Through whom e'en wicked men are
Thou com'st to share our misery, [blest
What can we render, Lord, to Thee!

Ah Lord, who hast created all, [small,
How hast Thou made Thee weak and
That Thou must choose Thy infant bed
Where ass and ox but lately fed!

Were earth a thousand times as fair,
Beset with gold and jewels rare,
She yet were far too poor to be
A narrow cradle, Lord, for Thee.

For velvets soft and silken stuff,
Thou hast but hay and straw so rough,
Whereon Thou king so rich and great,
As 'twere thy heaven, art throned in state.

Thus hath it pleased Thee to make plain
The truth to us poor fools and vain,
That this world's honour, wealth, and
    might,
Are nought and worthless in Thy sight.

Ah! dearest Jesus, Holy Child,
Make Thee a bed, soft, undefiled,
Within my heart, that it may be
A quiet chamber kept for Thee.

My heart for very joy doeth leap,
My lips no more can silence keep;
I too must raise with joyful tongue
That sweetest ancient cradle-song.

Glory to God in highest heaven,
Who unto man His Son hath given!

The angels joyes for to heir,
The gracious gift of this new yeir.

While angels sing with pious mirth
A glad New Year to all the earth.

I have no English version to exhibit of the next which I insert, but as it follows the other in the compendious book, I place it here along with the German original. The author of the German is not known. It appears in the Strassburg hymn-book of 1537.

To us is borne a bairne of blis,
Our King and Empriour,
Ane gracious Virgine mother is
To God hir Saviour.
Had not that blissit Bairne beene borne,
Wee had beene every ane forlorne,
With sinne and feindis fell.
Christ Jesus, loving bee to thee,
That thou ane man wold borne bee,
To saif us from the hell.

Ein kindelein so löbelich
Ist uns geboren heute
Von einer Jungfrau säuberlich
Zum trost uns armen leute.
Wär' uns das kindlein nicht gebor'n,
So wär'n wir allzumal verlor'n;
Das heil ist unser allen,
Ei, du süsser Jesu Christ,
Der du mensch geboren bist;
Behüt uns vor der holle.

Wee suld lufe God and mirrie bee,
And drive away dispair;
For Christ is cummit from hevin so hye,
Our fall for to repair.
No tongue sik kyndnesse can expresse,
The forme of servand taken hes,
And verbum caro factum est;
Except sinne, lyke vnto vs all,
To freith us from the feindis thrall,
And mend quhair wee did misse.

Der tag der is so freudenreich
Zu loben Gotes namen,
Dass Christus von den himmelreich
Auf erden zu uns kommen.
Gross ist die demuth und die gnad
Die Gott von himmel bei uns that;
Ein knecht ist er hie worden,
In allem, doch ohn' sünd uns gleich,
Dadurch wir werden ewig reich;
Trug unsrer sunde bürden.

For weill is them ever moir,
That trowis faithfullye,
Be grace to ring with Christ in gloir,
Throw faith alanerlie;
And weill is them that understude
The gratious gift of Christis blude,
Sched sinners for to win.

Wohl dem, der dieses glaubens ist,
Von gantzem hertzen trauet,
Dem wird die seligkeit gewiss:
Wohl dem der darauf bauet,
Dass g'nug fur uns that Jesus Christ,
Darum er ausgegangen ist,
Von Gott, dem ewigen Vater,

Wes hard never so kinde ane thing ;
Christ for his fais on croce did hing,
   To purge us from our sinne.

Thus thanke wee him full hertfully
   For his greit gentilnes :
Wee pray him, for his greit mercy,
   Trew preichours to incres ;
False Pharisianes and feinzeit lair,
Quhom wee have followit lait and air,
   Baith us and them forgeve ;
God, Father, Sonne, and Haly Spreit,
Instruct us in thy word so sweit,
   And after it to leve.

Owie so grosse wunderthat !
Christus trägt uns're missethat
   Und stillet unsrer hader.

Dess dank' ihm alle Christenheit
   Fur solche grosse güte ;
Und bitten sein' Barmherzigkeit,
   Dass er uns fort behüte,
Vor falscher lehr' und bösem wahn,
Der unsern seelen schaden kann ;
   Er woll' all schuld vergeben.
Gott, Vater, Sohn, und heil' ger Geist,
Wir bitten von dir allermeist :
   Lass uns in friede leben.

I cannot refrain from adding to these three hymns the wild lilt to which reference has already been made, and the short hymn on the resurrection of our Lord, which seems to be translated directly from the Latin. I cannot exhibit an English version of either, but yet I think the close correspondence will, through means of the Latin, be generally perceived. The first of these two hymns, as has been already mentioned, was composed in mediæval times, and the original had a stanza between the last two addressed to the Virgin Mary. In some of the German Protestant versions, as well as in the Scotch, this third stanza is simply omitted,* but in others its place is supplied by another stanza more accordant with Protestant ideas. The second of these hymns, as has been also mentioned, seems to have been more immediately derived from the Latin than from the German. The Latin is said to have been the composition of Hermann Bonn, and to have appeared in German hymn-books as early as 1542 or 1543.

In dulci jubilo, Now let vs sing with mirth and jo.
Our heartis consolation lyes in principio,†
And schynes as the sunne matris in gremio.
Alpha es & O.   Alpha es & O.

In dulci jubilo, Nun singet und seyd froh,
Unsers hertzen's wonne, liegt in præsepio,
Und leuchtet als die sonne, Matris in græmio,
Alpha es et O, Alpha es et O.

* In the Str. Lang hymn-book of 1537 and 1543.   † Typographical error for " pra epio."

O Iesu parvule, I thrist sore efter thee ; O Jesu parvule, Nach dir ist mir so weh,
Comfort my hart and minde. O puer optime, Tröst mir mein gemuthe, O puer optime,
God of all grace sa kind, et princeps gloriæ, Durch alle deine gute, O princeps gloriæ,
Trahe me post te, trahe me poste te. Trahe me post te, Trahe me post te.
Vbi sunt gaudia in ony place bot there, Ubi sunt gaudia, Nirgend mehr denn da
Quhair that the angels sing nova cantica, Da die Engel singen, Nova cantica,
Bot and the bellis ring in Regis curia ! Und die schellen klingen, in Regis curia,
God gif I were there; God gif I were there. Eia wären wir da, Eia wären wir da.

ANE SANG OF THE RESURRECTION.   DE MORTE ET RESURRECTIONE CHRISTI.

Christ gaue him selfe to die,   Christus pro nobis passus est
And for our fault the mendis made ;   Et immolatus agnus est,
For vs hee sched his precious blude,   Effuso suo sanguine
With greit triumph vpon the rude,   In ipsa crucis arbore,
And sinne and Sathan there hes slaine, Et mortuus imperium
And sauit vs fra hells paine.   Devicit diabolicum.

For hee againe from deid vp rais,   Nam resurgens ex mortuis
Victour of deid and all our fais ;   Victor redit ex inferis,
Hee raise the obligatioun,   Delevit et chirographum,
Contrair to our saluation :   Nobis quod est contrarium,
Syne spulzeit Sathan, hell and sinne, Exspoliato Satana
And heuinly gloir to vs hes win.   Reclusa cœli januâ.

And wee are now at God's peace,   Habemus ergo liberum
Throw Christ ressauit to his grace,   Jam nos ad Patris aditum,
Our Father mercifull is hee ;   Per Christum Dei filium
And we sall ring with him in blis.   Pro nobis morti traditum,
Allalua, allalua, benedicamus Domino. Alleluia Alleluia,
                        Benedicamus domino.*

* Perhaps the hymn in the second part of Wedderburn's book, entitled " Christe qui lux," is also
more immediately from the Latin than from the German, though I cannot speak with so much confidence
respecting it, as there seem to have been several German versions. I insert the first three verses of the
Scotch and Latin :

"Christ thou art the light but and the day,   " Christe, qui lux es et die
The mirkness of the night thou puttes away: Noctis tenebras detegis :
Wee knaw thou art the verie light   Lucisque lumen crederis,
That shynes to us baith day and night.   Lumen beatis prœdicans.

The next which I give at length, is from the second part of Wedderburn's book.   It is Weisse's hymn, which is still one of those sung in Germany at the burial of the dead ; and the fact that it was found appended to the funeral service used at the Kirk of Montrose in the latter half of the sixteenth century would seem to show that a similar use was made of it in that town, and probably elsewhere within the jurisdiction of the Superintendent of Angus.   It reflects in a striking manner the deep and tender pathos of the original.   That which is the eighth verse of the hymn in Miss Winkworth's translation was added in the German hymn-books about 1540.   Whether the additional verses of the Scotch are original or a later addition from some German form I have not been able as yet to ascertain.

BURIAL OF THE DEAD.

Our brother let us put in grave,
And na dout thereof let us have,
But hee sall rise on domise-day,
And have immortall life for aye.

Hee is of earth, and of earth made,
And man returne to earth againe;
Syne rise sall from the earth and ground,
When that the last trumpet sall sound.

The saull reignes with God in glore,
And hee sall suffer paine no more ;
For cause his faith was constantly
In Christes blude allenerly.

Now lay me calmly in the grave
This form, whereof no doubt we have
That it shall rise again that day,
In glorious triumph o'er decay.

And so to earth again we trust
What came from dust, and turns to dust,
And from the dust shall surely rise
When the last trumpet fills the skies.

His soul is living now in God
Whose grace his pardon hath bestowed,
Who through His Son redeem'd him here
From bondage unto sin and fear.

"O haly Lord, we thee beseik,
This night us to defend and keipe,
Thy rest and peace be with us all,
Let never na evill thing us befall.

"Na hevie sleepe nor deadly sinne,
Let not our enemie us ouercome,
Nor yet our flesh give na consent,
Grant us our faults for to repent."

"Precamur. sancte domine,
Defende nocte ac die,
Sit nobis in te requies,
Quietam noctem tribue.

"Ne gravis somnus inruat,
Nec hostis nos subripiat,
Nec illi consentiat,
Nec tibi reos statuat."

His painefull pilgrimage is past,
And till ane end cummit at the last,
Deiand in Christe's yocke full sweit,
Bot yet is livand in his spreit.

The saull levis with God, I say ;
The bodie sleipes whill domise-day :
Then Christ shall bring them both to glore,
To reigne with him for evermore.

In earth he had vexatioun,
But now he has salvatioun,
Reignand in glore and blisse but weir,
And shines as the sunne so cleire.

Yee faithfull therefore let him sleip,
And not like Heathen for him weip,
But deiply prent into your breist,
That deid to us approaches neist.

. . .

Christ, for thy might and celsitude,
That for our sinnes shed thy blude ;
Grant us in fayth to live and die,
And syne receiue our saules to thee.

His trials and his griefs are past,
A blessed end is his at last ;
He bore Christ's yoke, and did His will,
And though he died he liveth still.

He lives where none can mourn and weep,
And calmly shall this body sleep
Till God shall death himself destroy
And raise it into glorious joy.

He suffer'd pain and grief below,
Christ heals him now from all his woe ;
For him hath endless joy begun ;
He shines in glory like the sun.

Then let us leave him to his rest,
And homeward turn, for he is blest,
And we must well our souls prepare,
When death shall come, to meet him there.

So help us, Christ, our Hope in loss !
Thou hast redeem'd us by Thy cross
From endless death and misery ;
We praise, we bless, we worship Thee !

The last of which I deem it necessary to give the Scotch and an English version at length is the metrical rendering of the " Gloria in Excelsis," attributed to the German poet Decius. I prefer in this instance to give an old English translation. Both versions vary farther from the original than those of the hymns previously given, but still it is evident enough that they are versions of one original ;* and, singularly enough, an examination of the original and of this old English translation of it, enables us to correct some typographical errors which have crept into Wedderburn's version.

---

* Both agree with the German in several things in which it differs from the older version of the " Gloria in excelsis."

DECIUS' HYMN. | GLORIA IN EXCELSIS DEO.

Onlie to God on heich bee gloir,
And loving bee unto his grace :
Quha can condempne us ony moir,
Sen wee are now at Godis peace ?
Intill his fauour wee are tane,
Throw faith in Jesus Christ allane,
Be quhome his wrath sall end and ceis.

To God the hyghest be glory alwaye,
For his great kyndnesse and mercy ;
That doth provyde both nyght and daye
Both for oure soule and oure body.
To mankynde hath God great pleasure,
Now is great peace every where ;
God hath put out all emmyte.

Wee worship, and wee love and praise
Thy majesty and magnitude ;
That thow, God, Father only wise,
Rings over all with fortitude :
No toung can tell thy strength nor micht,
Thy words and thochtis all are richt,
And all thy warkes just and gude.

We love and prayse and honoure the,
For thy great glory ; we thanke thy grace,
That thou, God, Father eternally,
Art oure defender in every place.
Thou art to us a mercyfull Father,
And we thy chyldren altogether ;
Therfore we geve the thankes alwayes.

Lord Jesus Christ, Sonne only borne,
Of thy Father celestiall ;
Thou savit us that was forlorne,
From sin and hell, and sathanis thrall.
Lord God's Lambe, thou tuke on thee,
For all our sinne to satisfie.
Lord bee mercifull to us [all].

O Jesu Christ, thou onely Sonne
Of God Almyghty thy heavenly Father,
Our full and whole redempcyon,
Thou that hast stilled God's displeasure ;
O God's Lambe, that takest synne awaye,
When we have nede, helpe us alwaye ;
Graunt us thy mercy altogether.

O Holy Ghaist, our comfort gude,
From feindis feill thy flock defend,
[Quhilk Christ redeemit with his blude,]
To thy keiping wee them commend,
From errour and hypocrisie,
Strenth us in the victorie, [veritie]
To persevir unto the end.

O Holy Ghoost, our comfortoure
In all oure trouble and hevynesse ;
Defende us all from Sathan's power,
Whome Christ hath bought from woful-
    nesse :
Kepe oure hertes in the verite,
In oure tentacyon stonde us by,
And strength alwaye oure weake bodies.

Taking away the word within brackets at the end of the last line of
the third stanza of the Scotch version, it will be seen that that line is left

a syllable shorter than the last lines of the other stanzas, and does not rhyme with the fourth line as in the others. I conclude, therefore, that a word has fallen away, and that the word is the one I have supplied in brackets, both because that word corrects the irregularities and makes the translation an exact rendering of the German original "Erbarm' dich unser *aller*." Farther, it will be observed that, without the line in brackets, the fourth stanza of the Scotch version is a line shorter than the other three, and that there is no line to rhyme with the first as the third does in the previous stanzas. I therefore venture to supply the line included in brackets, which removes these irregularities, and is a pretty faithful expression of the idea contained in two lines of the origi- nal, "Die Jesus Christ erlöset, durch grosse martr'r und bittern todt." The word "veritie" is given as a conjectural emendation for "victorie," as it makes a more intelligible meaning, and is used in the old English version of this hymn. There are several other cases in which a refer- ence to the German original enables us to correct typographical errors in the Scotch book, and two or three cases in which it enables us to supply a missing line. The occurrence of such serious errors in the book rather countenances the idea that it must have been printed when its author was not at hand to revise the proofs, and probably from a hastily tran- scribed manuscript.

I have referred above to an old English translation of the hymn just quoted. This is contained in the "Ghostly Psalms and Spiritual Songs of Myles Coverdale," lately reprinted among his other works by the Parker Society. This treatise bears *in gremio* even less acknowledgment of its being a translation than the Scotch book of godly and spiritual songs, though it is more exclusively so, and though, in another part of the volume, the Editor gives a list of Coverdale's works by Bishop Bale, from which it appears that he translated "Cantiones Wittenber- gensium," Lib. i.. yet, in the long note which he prefixes to the treatise, he gives no hint in his preface that the Psalms and Songs were translations from the German, and were, in fact, the "cantiones" referred to by Bale. Such, however, is the undoubted fact with respect to them,' and the arrangement and contents of the treatise correspond with the Wittemberg hymn-books, while the Scotch translation in these respects corresponds more closely with the German hymn-books issued elsewhere. Still the two have a number of hymns in common, the comparison of which affords a very satisfactory means of determining the merits of the respective translators. But what is even more remarkable is, that four hymns, exactly or almost exactly alike, appear in both treatises, and it is a very difficult question to determine which of the translators must have borrowed these from the other. In favour of the claim of Coverdale to be the original translator of these is the averment that his treatise had been published by the year 1539, and that there is no reason to suppose the Scotch translation was published so early, nor perhaps the particular German hymn-book from which it was taken. In favour of the opinion that the Scotch is the original, stands the fact that these hymns are superior to most of the others translated by Coverdale, and that the Scotchman is known to have been the better poet of the two, and the farther fact that several of the minor changes made on them seem to be more easily accounted for on this supposition than on the other. But however this may be settled, there is not the slightest doubt that the one must have borrowed from the other, and that it is just possible that even before the year 1539 Coverdale had been brought into contact with Wedderburn's friends, Alesius and Machabæus, if not even with Wedderburn himself. Alan or Alesius, like Coverdale, was a protegé of Lord Cromwell's, and for some time before he went to Germany was employed by him in helping forward the cause of the Reformation in England. M'Alpine or Machabæus was for some years settled in the south of England, and boldly taught the reformed doctrines there; and as Coverdale was similarly employed for part of the time in one of the neighbouring counties, and shortly after became brother-in-law to Machabæus, it is not at all unlikely that their long and steady friendship had begun even before 1539. Even then if there really were more foundation than has been shown for the statement that the first edition of Coverdale's hymns was issued in 1539, and that these four hymns were contained in that edition, it is not altogether impossible that he may have got them from one of these Scotchmen, and that the thoughts of Wedderburn, as well as those of his elder brother, may have already been turned towards the work he afterwards executed. But this edition of Coverdale's Psalms and Songs is admitted to bear no date, and contains a translation of one hymn which is not known to have appeared in Germany till the year 1540; and the supposition that any edition of the book was printed in 1539, rests entirely on the fact that it was included in a list of prohibited books given under that year in the first edition of Foxe's Acts and Monuments. But this list is not given in the second and some subsequent editions of Foxe, and the most recent and accurate editor* of that great work states explicitly that it was not issued till 1546, and that this can still be ascertained from Bishop Bonner's register, which contains the Act of prohibition and the list of prohibited books. Long before that date Coverdale had himself fled to Germany, had become the brother-in-law of M'Alpine, and had, it can hardly be doubted, met with the other Scotchmen at Wittenberg. I shall exhibit, in an Appendix, some of these hymns in the form in which they are given both by Wedderburn and by Coverdale, from which it will be at once perceived that, with a few very trifling exceptions, there are no farther differences than that the one uses the English and the other the Scotch form of certain words. The first I give is the beautiful German hymn, "Herr Christ der einig Gottes Sohn," which still holds its place in the modern collections, and of which a partial translation into modern English has been given by Miss Winkworth. At least other three correspond nearly as closely in all respects. These are the translations of Psalm lxvii. and of the Magnificat, both of which I have placed in the Appendix, and the hymn, "Ich ruf' zu dir Herr Jesu Christ," which, as it is included in my third Appendix, I do not insert in the first. The only farther difference between the two translators with respect to this last hymn is that Wedderburn puts the seventh and eighth lines of the German stanza into one line. I exhibit here the translations both have given of Psalm cxxx., because, though the differences between them

* Townsend's "Foxe," Vol. v., pp. 565, 566, and Appendix No. XVIII. The Psalms and Songs are not found even in the list of prohibited books issued in 1542, and given in Appendix No. X. of same volume; so that the recent editor of Coverdale seems to have made a mistake in asserting on the strength of the above list that his hymns were published by 1539. He tells us that Coverdale's wife was of Scotch extraction, while Dr Lorimer tells us that the wife of M'Alpine was an Englishwoman.

E

are greater, they evidently draw from a common source, and that source
a modification of Luther's version of this Psalm not given in my hymn
books. This Psalm, besides, is one of the most favourable specimens of
Coverdale's powers as a translator:

WEDDERBURN.	COVERDALE.
Fra deip (O Lord) I call on thee,	Out of the depe cry I to thee,
Lord, heir my invocatioun,	O Lorde, Lorde, hear my callynge;
Thy eiris thou incline to me,	O let thyne eares enclyned be
And heir my lamentatioun :	To the voyce of my complaynynge.
For gif thou will our sin impute	If thou, Lord, wilt deal with stratenesse,
Till us, O Lord, that we commit,	To marke all that is done amysse,
Wha may bide thy accusation.	Lord, who may abyde thy reckonynge?
Bot thow art mercifull and kinde,	But there is mercy ever with thee,
And hes promittet in thy write,	That thou therefore mayst be feared;
Them that repent with heart and minde	I will abyde the Lord patiently;
Of all their sin to make them quite.	My soul looketh for him unfaynted,
Thocht I be full of sinfulnes,	And in his word is all my trust;
Yit thow art full of faithfulnes,	So is my hope and comforte most,
And thy promise trew and perfyte.	His promise shall be fulfylled.
My hope is stedfast in the Lord,	As the watchemen in the mornynge
My saull ever on him traist,	Stonde lokynge longe desyrously;
And my beleve is in thy word,	That they myght see the faire daysprynge;
And all thy promises maist and leist.	So waytteth my soul for the Lord dayly.
My saull on God waites, and is bent,	Therefore let Israel wayte styll,
As watchman would the night were went,	Until it be the Lorde's wyll,
Bydand the day to take him rest.	To lowse them from adversité.
Israel, in God put thy beliefe,	For with the Lord, there is mercy,
For hee is full of gentilnes,	And great plenteous redempcyon;
Freedome, gudnes, and sall releve	Allthough we synne oft wickedly,
All Israel of their distres.	Yet hath he for us a sure pardon.
Hee sall deliver Israell,	He shall redeme poore Israel,
And all their sinnes sall expell	And him shall he delyver full well
And claith them with his righteousnesse.	From all the synnes that he hath done.

As Bale, in his brief notice of Coverdale, has preserved for us the knowledge of the fact that he made a translation of the Wittenberg hymns, so Calderwood has preserved for us in his short notice of John Wedderburn a record of the fact that he made translations of Luther's hymns. True he does not expressly say that these translations were inserted in "the booke of godly and spiritual sangs," any more than Bale distinctly identifies the ghostly psalms and spiritual songs of Coverdale with his translation of the Wittenberg hymns; nor does he in fact make express mention of the compendious book at all, but with the facts, which he supplies, set distinctly before us, and compared with those I have already given, no one can hesitate to make the identification for himself. Calderwood's notice of the Wedderburns was not embodied in the shorter form of his history which, for nearly two hundred years, was the only one printed; and the last editor of their collection who consulted the larger manuscript which the Wodrow Society has since printed, was so far from catching a glimpse of the meaning of Calderwood's statement, "he translated into Scottish metre the dytements of Luther," that he changed the uncouth Scottish word, "dytements" for another which does not suggest the same idea at all, and told us simply that Wedderburn translated the *principles of Luther into Scottish verse.*[*] This, and the circumstance that most of our recent ecclesiastical historians had begun their study of Calderwood before the new edition of his history was published, may probably account for the fact that his statement had attracted so little notice that only one—the most accurate and laborious Dr Lorimer—seems to have adverted to it at all, and even he but repeats without remark what he found in Calderwood. That historian had probably received his information from oral tradition, or had made but a very perfunctory examination of the facts, for though so large a proportion of J. Wedderburn's hymns are translations from the German, less than the half of these are actually from Luther: and besides, the psalms, even with fewer exceptions than the hymns, are translations from some pre-existent work. This fact, though most explicitly acknowledged in the compendious book, as has been already stated, appears to have been overlooked both by Calderwood, Dr Lorimer,* and others who have directed attention to that work. In Appendix III. I give in parallel columns several of the Scotch godly and spiritual songs and the German hymns of which I suppose them to be translations, and I add three or four of the Scotch versions of the Psalms, and the German versions which they appear to resemble, that any German scholar may be able to satisfy himself of the close connection existing between the two. I do not include in this appendix those which I have inserted in my Lecture, because the fact of the resemblance of the Scotch to the English, which last is professedly a translation from the German, must determine the character and origin of these particular hymns.

I have not as yet met with any one German hymn-book containing all the hymns translated by Wedderburn, or having a large proportion of them, in the same order. Those in Wackernagel's "Bibliographie" that bear the closest resemblance to his collection are the Strassburg hymn-books from 1537 to 1547, and the Magdeburg hymn-book of 1543. The Leipsic hymn-book of 1552 contains the first five of the selected psalms in nearly the same order, and also the articles of the catechism, but in other respects has no marked resemblance. The Magdeburg book contains very nearly all the psalms and hymns found in the Scotch book, and it was one of the first that exhibited the several articles of the catechism in the exact order in which they are given by our countryman. The Strassburg hymn-books, from 1537 downwards, contain most of the psalms and hymns he has translated, and all, with three or four exceptions, are there by 1545. The psalms awanting may of course be found in the Strassburg Psalter. A prologue of somewhat similar form to that of Wedderburn, and containing a somewhat similar translation of Col. iii. 16, is found in the Strassburg books. The error as to the numbering of Psalm lxxix. occurs also in them.†

Great exception has been taken both in former times and in our own to the ballads in the "compendious book," and a sort of mingled con-

---

* Calderwood's words are, "H. translated many of Luther's dytements into Scottish metre, and the Psalms of David." Lorimer's statement is, "He became a zealous reformer, and translated many of Luther's hymns and of the Psalms of David into Scottish metre."—(Scot. Ref. p. 174.)
† Wackernagel's Das Deutsche Kirchenlied p. 355. Bibliographie p. 201.

tempt and pity expressed for those who could find pleasure in them, and encourage the repeated publication of them. They who have given expression to such opinions forget that a similar adaptation of the tunes, and even, to some extent, of the words of secular songs, was made in the same age in Germany, France, and Holland; and that even in a much later age, one of whose deep piety and true poetic taste there can be no question raised, seemed to vindicate the lawfulness of the practice when he complained that so much of the best music we had should be tamely given up to the service of the devil. It is a well-known fact that the tunes of many of the finest German hymns, in so far as they were not founded on those of the old Latin ones, were taken from secular songs; even the very names of which would, but for this, have been now forgotten. Not unfrequently with the melody, the words were also partially appropriated,* and notwithstanding all that has been said in condemnation of the practice, it may be doubted whether, from the countenance it has received from hymn writers of acknowledged eminence, any other criterion can be laid down on the subject than that such appropriations are not to be made rashly, nor indiscriminately, nor farther than the general feeling of the age or country is prepared to acquiesce in them. But whatever may be thought of this practice, it will not at least be denied that it was far more venial, and indicative of a higher, more earnest, and praiseworthy taste than the practice which was so common among our countrymen in the times immediately preceding, of adapting the tunes of the church hymns to secular, and sometimes very profane songs, and singing these at certain seasons, even in the house of God,† as well as in their households, and at their social gatherings. To those who take exception to the character and spirit of the satirical ballads, rather than to the fact of their being adaptations of secular songs and tunes to sacred subjects, it may perhaps be sufficient to reply that no one ought to blame them too severely in these respects who does not know something of those they were intended to supersede, and did to a large extent succeed

---

* For instance, the German hymn, "O welt ich muss dich lassen," was but the echo of the plaintive ballad "Innsbruck ich muss dich lassen;" and even one of the drinking songs had been spiritualized by a Roman Catholic, as well as by a Protestant poet.　　　　† Abp. Hamilton's Catechism.

in superseding, and no one who does know these others will fail to own
that a great moral and religious triumph was secured when they were
superseded by others so much more pure and elevating.   The passage
from them to Wedderburn's is almost as from darkness to light, from
filth and ribaldry to comparative modesty, refinement, and earnest religious principle.   In fact, one has only cursorily to compare them even
with the plays of Sir David Lindsay, acted before the noble lords and
ladies of the court of Scotland, to discover how far in advance of the best
in that era the earnest men who had lived in the atmosphere of Wittenberg, where Protestantism had already had time to shew its effects,
were in point of true refinement, gentleness, and modesty.   Then one
has only carefully to compare them with similar compositions published
about the same time in England, France, and Germany, to satisfy himself that if there was one of the ballad writers of the age who cherishes
a less bitter remembrance of mere personal wrongs, and a less unchristian
spirit towards those who had inflicted them, than the rest, it is the twice-
exiled author of most of these "Godly Ballads." True there are
stanzas in them, just as there are sentences in Knox's history, which be-
tray the coarseness of the olden time, and they do speak of popery and
its priests in a style very different from that which would now be used.
But we speak in cool blood, and have to do with men of higher moral
culture, while the authors of these ballads wrote in the very crisis of a
life and death struggle* between truth and error, between purity and
debauchery, to support and cheer those who were contending even unto
bonds, imprisonment, and death, for the simplicity and purity of the gospel.   If their rude songs and homely earnest words commended themselves to the hearts of such, and encouraged them and their associates to

---

* I can find but one reference in the "Godly and Spiritual Songs" which I can confidently adduce as
shewing how deeply the author felt his exile from his native land :—

Allone I weepe in great distress.
We are exilit remedelesse.
  And wait not why
Fra God's word, allace, allace.
  Uncourteouslie.

They may our bodie fra thee bind,
So can they not our hertes and minde,
  Fixed on thee,
Howbeit we be with dolour pined
  Uncourteouslie.

continue the exhausting struggle till their cause was crowned with victory,
their authors did a signal service to their country, which ought to be
more gratefully remembered and less grudgingly acknowledged than it
has ever yet been.   Many of their compositions are as truly martyrs'
and confessors' songs as any of those of the Covenanters in the succeeding century.   A short specimen or two of their authors' yearning tenderness towards their deluded fellow countrymen, and of their hearty efforts
even for the reformation of those priests whom they felt it so necessary to
denounce, is all for which I can here make room.   The first I give is from
one of the ballads, which I suppose must be an original composition.

Priests, worship God,	Priests, prove yow men,
And put away imagerie,	And now defend your liberty :
Your pardons and fraternitie,	For France and for your dignitie,
To hell, the way and road.	Yee brake the peace yee ken.
Priests, sell no masse,	Priests, now confesse,
Bot minister that sacrament,	How yee so lang did us begyle,
As Christ, in the New Testament,	With many haly bellie wyle,
Commandit you express.	To live in idleness.
Priests, change your tune,	I yow exhort,
And sing into your mother tongue	Your office to do perfite ;
English Psalms, an' ye impugn ;	*For I say nothing in despite.*
Ye dine after noone.	So God mot me support.

The second specimen I give, I must confess to be in the main a translation of a German hymn, but it is a translation which breathes quite as
kindly and compassionate a spirit towards the deluded Papists as the
original, and displays a tone and temper considerably different from that
which even Coverdale has managed to throw into his version of the same
hymn.

WEDDERBURN.	COVERDALE.
" Our bairnis now weill knawis how	" It is so cleare, as we may heare,
To worship God with service trew,	No man by ryght can it deny,
Quhilkst mony year our fathers deir,	That many a year thy people deare
Allace ! therefore, full sore misknew.	Have been begyled per'lously

Yet God did feed his chosen indeed,
  As Noy and Lot and mony moe,
And had respect to his elect
  However the blind warld did goe.

" Sen throw thy strenth thy word at
  Is preachit cleir before our eine, [lenth
Bee yet gude Lord, misericord
  To them quhilk yet dissavit bein,
And not dois knaw but mennis law
  To their greit damnatioun ;
Teich them fra hand to understand
  Thy word to their salvatioun."

With men spiritual, as we them call,
  But not of thy Spirite truly ;
For more carnall are none at all
  Than many of these spirites be.

" They have been ever sworne altogether
  Their owne laws for to keep alwaye :
But, merciful Lord, of thy sweet worde
  There durst no man begin to saye.
They durst them call great heretics all
  That did confesse it steadfastly ;
For they chargéd it should be hid,
  And not be spoken of openly."

The metrical versions of the psalms contained in the second part of the compendious book, and which some have pronounced to be so superior to the rest of its contents, appear to me, I must confess, to be in general the least successful part of the whole collection. No doubt there are stanzas which deserve to live even in them, particularly in the 23d, the 124th, and the 130th, but the mass of them would never, without the hymns and ballads which accompany them, have taken such a hold on the minds of our forefathers. In fact almost the only one which seems to have taken a deep hold on their minds, and the stanza and even some of the words of which were retained in Knox's Psalter is the paraphrase, and (if one might safely settle such a point on internal grounds, without an exhaustive search through the whole of the old German hymn books,) I should be disposed to add the, in great measure, original paraphrase of Psalm lxxxiii.* With considerable poetic power and copiousness of imagery it exhibits a less restrained and chastened spirit than almost any even of the ballads, though one can easily understand how it should have gone to the hearts of men who believed, as they believed their own existence, that the cause for which they dared and suffered so much was the cause of God and truth, and that opponents strove to crush it as well as them.

* What is one line in Wedderburn is divided into two in Knox's Psalter, so that the stanza consists of fourteen instead of seven lines, just as in the case of Beza's stanza and tune for Psalm cxxiv, each line of the French is divided into two in the Scotch version. The translation of Psalm lxxxiii. in Knox's Psalter is much closer to the prose version than Wedderburn's, and is said to have been executed by Robert Pont, a native Scotchman, who could not fail to have been familiar with the other.

The hymns and other compositions in the first part of the Wedder-burns' book, though mostly, as I have already said, translations, are translations of some of the finest hymns which the Reformation gave to the Church, whose winning, life-like exhibition of its doctrines largely contributed to prepare the way for the first acceptance of them, and has continued to commend them to the hearts of German Protestants to the present day. They are translations executed with spirit, freedom, and true poetic taste into the purest Scottish dialect of the time, and they had the highest testimony accorded to their worth in the fact that with-out the sanction of the Church either unreformed or reformed they made their way to the hearts and households of the Scottish people, and con-tinued to be circulated, committed to memory, and sung in Scotland long after the circumstances which originally called them forth had passed away, while the more homely translations of a number of the same hymns into English by good old Coverdale appear to have had comparatively a very limited circulation and influence among the English people. The doctrinal teaching which pervades these hymns is on the whole wonder-fully like that which from the first has prevailed in the Reformed Church of Scotland, and the only way of salvation for sinners of our guilty race is set forth with singular clearness, and returned to in almost every hymn with a persistency which nothing but the author's hearty and loving acceptance of it can explain. Still, on some minor points, there are such differences as tend to shew that the author had studied in the school of Germany rather than in that of Geneva, or that his poems belong theo-logically to the earlier era of the Reformation. Dr. Bonar is, perhaps, right in supposing that there is nothing very distinctively or narrowly Lutheran in the hymns respecting baptism and the Lord's Supper, though these are unquestionably free translations of Luther's hymns. But in the long paraphrase of Psalm li., the first and second verses of which are said to have been sung by Wishart on an occasion already referred to, there occur expressions in regard to the general effects of baptism stronger than most Scottish Protestants would now use :—

Thou wyshe me, Lord, when I was borne,   But yet the Lord omnipotent.
  From all my wickedness ;   My cairfull case did cure,
But yet I did throw sin forlorne   *At font* when I was impotent
  Of hevin the righteousness,   Fragill, vain, vylde and pure ;
Wash me again, and from thy horne   Then helpit me that king potent,
  Deliver me in stress :   In my misaventure.*

.   .   .   .

Then a more distinct place of special honour is assigned to our Lord's
mother than is now usual among us, as where it is said in one of the
finest of the ballads after celebrating the praises of our Redeemer:

> Nixt Him to lut his Mother fair,
> With stedfast hert for evermair ;
> Scho bure the birth freed us from cair.†

And in another of the ballads, the local descent of our Saviour's soul
to hell between his death and resurrection is asserted, and the doctrine
that he then rescued a number of the spirits in prison and carried them
in triumph with him to heaven, is connected with a traditionary statement
of their number, apparently, but erroneously resting on Psalm lxviii. 17,
which interpretation of that verse I do not remember to have met with
elsewhere :

> Sanct John did tell, thou heryit hell,
>   And shew mercy.
> Ane thousand score thou did restore
>   To thy glory.‡

Some slips as to biblical facts are made by the author, as when in the
paraphrase of Psalm li.§ he speaks of Isaac as Abraham's eldest son.
The substitution of Mount Sinay for Mount Sion, in the version of the
Second Psalm, is probably but a typographical error, as it is not found in
the German hymn of which that version is in part a translation.

I have already said that several of the hymns and some of the Psalms
though confessedly translations, are translations executed with considerable
spirit, freedom, and poetic taste. Most of them contain figures and
similes which are evidently the translator's own, and some of these which
are evidently suggested by the original are treated in such a way as to

* Dalyell's Compendious Booke, pp. 112, 114.   † Ibid. p. 130.   ‡ Ibid. p. 123.   § Ibid. p. 114.

shew the author was not a mere versifier likes Myles Coverdale, but a true poet, whose words were fitted to go deep into the hearts of his countrymen, to rouse them to deeds of noble daring, and sustain them even under severest suffering. This cannot be better exemplified than by subjoining the translations which both have given of Psalm cxxiv. :—

(WEDDERBURN.)

Except the Lord with us had stand,
Had not the Lord been our warrand,
Say furth Israel unfeinzetly,
When men upraise in our countrey,
They had us all on live devored,
With ire so sharply they us shored,
   So kendled was their cruelty.

For like the water and wallés bryme,*
   They had ouerwhelméd us with might,
Like burnés that in spait fast rin,
   They had ouerthrawne us with slight
The bulrand streamés of their pryde
Had perished us throw back and syde,
   And reft fra us our life full right.

But loving to the Lord alone,
   That gave us nocht to be their prey,
To be rent with their teeth anone,
   But hes us freed full weill them fra.
Like to ane bird tane in ane net,
The whilk the fowler for her set,
   Sa is our life weill win away.

The net is broken in pieces small,
   And we are savit fra their shame,
Our hope was aye and ever sall
   Be in the Lord and in His name,
The whilk hes creat hevin sa hie,
And made the eird so marvelouslie,
   And all the ferlies of the same.

     * Waves furious.

COVERDALE.

Except the Lord had been with us,
   Now may Israel say boldly ;
Except the Lorde had been with us,
   When men rose up against us fiercely;
They had devoured us quyck doubtlesse,
And had overwoune us comfortlesse
   They were so wroth at us truly.

The waves of waters had wrapped us in ;
   Our soul had gone under the floode.
The deep waters of these proud men
   Had ronne our soules over, where they
     stoode.
The Lord be praysed every houre,
That wold not suffer them us to devoure,
   Nor in their teeth to sucke our bloode.

Our soule is delyvered from their power,
   They cannot have that they have sought,
As the byrde from the snare of the fouler,
   So are we from their dangers brought.
The snare is broken and we are free ;
Our helpe is in the Lorde's name truly,
   Which hath made heavin and earth of
     nought.

How much more pithily and forcibly the Scottish poet can express himself may be seen by the versions both have given of Psalm cxxxvii., and especially of its last verse. The word in it generally rendered stone might be more literally rendered, as in the German, rock, for which Wedderburn in that passage employs the old Scotch word "craig."* The same word is employed by him as the equivalent of the same original term in Psalm cxiv. where vers. 6, 7, 8 are thus rendered:

> " What gart yow mountaines, like rams stert and stend,
> And ye hills, like lambes loup and bend?
> It was the Lord's feir that made sic reird,
> And Jacob's God perturbit all the eird.
> For God turnit the craig in fresh river,
> The barren brae in fontaine water cleir."

This and the version given just before of Psalm cxxiv., though translations, seem to shew that the poet had been no inattentive observer of the scenery of the highland district of his native county with its bare braes and craigs, its mountain burns and rocky streams, "bulrand" and hurrying on with sudden " spaits," and occasionally dashing wildly over a linn to which last he alludes in his translation of Psalm lxxix., though there is no such allusion in the German version which in the main he follows:

> " And as water that fast rinnes ouer a lin,
> Dois not returne again to the awin place,
> Sa thow, gude Lord, put our sin from thy face."

One other simile must not be omitted in this notice. It is a peculiarly Scottish one, founded on a practice in our law which was often put in force against the early reformers and their successors. It is referred to in the verse quoted from the translation of Psalm li., and again in the following lines from one of the hymns on the birth of Christ:

---

* It is well known that Luther and some of the ablest German critics of our own day translate Psalm xxxvii. 37 in a manner different from that in which it is translated in the French and English prose and metrical versions of the Psalms. That translation is substantially adopted by Wedderburn:

> ' Keepe justice, and have ane eye unto the right,
> That sall make peace for ever with God of might.'

> " For ye were all at Godis horne,
>   This babe to you that now is born,
>   Sall make you safe and for you die,
>   And you restore to libertie."

I cannot refrain from giving one more illustration of the forcible and pithy manner in which this old Scottish poet can translate a passage which has not always been happily rendered by subsequent versifiers of the Psalms. It is from Psalm cxv. which the Compendious Book, following in this the Vulgate, makes a part of the preceding one instead of a separate composition :

> " Our God forsuith rings in heaven full hie,
>   And what him listis, or lykes, workes hee.
>   Their images of stock, stane, gilt with gold,
>   Are made be men, and syne for money sold.
>   They have a mouth can nother say nor sing ;
>   Their eene are blind and they can see nothing,
>   They cannot hear though men do cry and yell,
>   Their nosethirles can nother saver nor smell.
>   They have hands can nother feel nor grope
>   Their fundyit feet can nother gang nor loupe.
>   They can pronounce no voice furth of their throats,
>   They are ouergane with mouse-wobs and (with) motes."

Nor can I deny myself the pleasure of adding to these many extracts from the "booke of godly and spiritual sangs," one most favourable specimen of its merits and manner, which I have found no reason to believe is a translation of any pre-existent poem, and which I fondly hope will not hereafter be found to be so. Were there no other, (and there are many others distinguished by earnest moral purpose, deep and genuine love to the simple truths of the gospel and firm resolution to venture all in the maintenance and profession of them) this one, it appears to me, would have gone far to secure the authors' influence in those or in any days. I give it in a slightly abridged form:

" Say weill is throughly a worthy thing ;
  Of say weill great vertew forth does spring ;
  Say weill from do weill differs in letter ;
  Say weill is gude, bot do weill is better.

" Say weill is repute be man sum deale ;
  But do weill only to God does appeale :
  Say weill sayis godly, and mony does please ;
  But do weill lives godly, and does the world ease.

" Be saying weill, mony to God's word clevis ;
  But for lack of do weill, it quickly levis :
  Bot gif say weill and do weill were joynt in a frame,
  All were done, all were won, gotten were the game.

" Say weill in danger of deith is cald ;
  Do weill is harneist and wondrous bald :
  When say weill for fear sall tremble and quake ;
  Do weill sall be jocund and jolly cheere make.

" Say weill is slippar and makes mony wyles ;
  Do weill is seemly without any gyles ;
  Quhen say weill at sumtimes sall be broght base,
  Do weill sall triumph in every place.

" Say weill to silence sumtime is bound ;
  Do weill is free in every stound :
  Say weill hes friends baith here and there ;
  But do weill is welcome every where.

" Say weill many things in hand does take ;
  Do weill ane end of them does make :
  When say weill with mony is quite down-cast
  Do weill is trusty and will stand fast.

" Say weill, mony will be sa kind ;
  But do weill few will unto their friend :
  May say weill, then do weill I tell you indeed,
  But do weill is mair honest in time of need.

In conclusion, I may perhaps be allowed to say a few words in reply to those who ask me what good I hope to accomplish by calling attention to these long forgotten songs, and why I think it worth while to devote so much time to the elucidation of their history. I have done so, first, because the facts I have succeeded in ascertaining seem to me to go a good way to determine the substantial worth of this favourite book of our fathers, and to justify attention to certain parts of its contents which former investigators have very generally overlooked ; and, secondly, because the facts ascertained seem to me to cast some light on certain points connected with the Scottish Reformation. Historical research in recent times had rather tended to show that the Reformers of Wittenberg had not had so entirely the moulding of the precursors of Knox as had been at one time supposed ; and no doubt it must now be admitted that Wishart's teaching is to be more closely identified with the Swiss than with the German Confession. But if any reliance can be placed on the conclusions to which I have thought myself warranted to come, it may still be said that, though our reformers very early took their form of doctrine from Switzerland, the country in which that subject was most calmly and thoroughly investigated, yet, as they drew their chief encouragement to contend for the free circulation of the inspired Word of God from the able and persistent appeals of one of the most accomplished pupils of Luther and Melanchthon, so they drew the spirit which nerved them to persevere in the contest, and cheered them amidst all its hardships, from another of the noble band of Scottish exiles who was trained under the same honoured teachers, and imbued with their own earnestness and deep love of sacred song. In fact, Scotland was, perhaps with the exception of Switzerland itself, the only country where the hymns of Germany and the doctrines of Calvin circulated side by side, and for long retained in common their living hold on the people. Lastly, I have thought it worth while to do so because, at a time when so many are acquiring a knowledge of the German language for the purposes of their profession, whether secular or sacred, and may thereby meet with books in it which have a tendency to sap the foundations of their faith, I think it is specially necessary to remind them that there are in the same language an immense collection of noble hymns,— perhaps the richest treasury of devotion the Christian Church has yet received—from whose stores our fathers drew for their enrichment and godly edifying in the truth as it is in Jesus—from whose stores many weary and anxious spirits have in later times drawn light and life and comfort and courage, and by use of which many honoured brethren in the German churches have been preserved from making shipwreck of faith, and many have been drawn back to the good old paths from which at one time they had gone astray. If it be true, as Sir Roundell Palmer has so beautifully said, that the hymns of the Church are virtually the liturgy of the laity, and as another has hinted, that their liturgy is virtually their confession, there is no collection of hymns which, for variety and copiousness, for fulness and yet simplicity of evangelical statement, for richness and yet chasteness of imagery and sentiment, is once to be compared with that which the Reformation gave to the German churches. The fact that this collection, to a very considerable extent, grew out of, and gathered up into itself all that was truest and best of the older Latin, may perhaps incline us to look on the Reformation as something else than a narrow or negative movement, and impress on us the much-needed lesson, that in order to hold our place in the orderly march of the Christian host it is quite as necessary to hold fast by the good and true which has been already attained as to reach forth after that which yet remains to be won. To those who can do so, I say, make acquaintance with this treasury of devotion in the German original; to those who cannot do this I say, make acquaintance with it in the form in which Miss Winkworth and others have so fully laid it open to the British people, if not in the ruder form in which Wedderburn commended it to our fathers. "That these hymns first sprang up on a foreign soil is no reason why they should not take root among us." "Any embodiment of Christian experience and devotion, whether in the form of hymn, or prayer, or meditation, or whatever shape art may give it, if it do but go right to the heart of our common faith, becomes at once the rightful and most precious inheritance of the whole Christian Church. Much more, then, when the country is so nearly akin to our own, may we feel that it is at once our privilege and our duty to appropriate all that she can bestow on us," and endeavour that her gifts may "find a welcome and a home" in our own land.

APPENDIX.

I.

(Wedderburn.)　　　　　　　　*(Coverdale.)*

Christ is the onely Sonne of God,
The Father eternall :
We haue in Jesse found the rode,
God and man naturall.
Hee is the morning star;
His beemis send hee out hes far
Beyond other sternis all.

Hee was for vs ane man borne,
In the last part of time;
Yet keipit shee her maid-heid vnforlorne,
His Mother that bure him; syne
Hee hes helles yettes broken,
And heuin hee hes made oppen,
Bringand vs life againe.

Thou only Maker of all thing,
Thou euerlasting light,
From end to end all rewling,
Be thy owne godly might;
Turne thow our hertes vnto thee,
And lighten them with the veritie,
That are far from the ryght.

Let vs incres in loue of thee,
And in knowledge also.

Christ is the only Sonne of God,
The Father eternall;
We have in Jesse founde this rod,
God and man naturall;
He is the mornynge star;
His beames sendeth he out farre,
Beyonde other starres all.

He was for us a man borne
In the last part of tyme;
Yet kepte the maydenheade unforlorne
His Mother that bare hym :
He hath hell gates broken,
And heauen hath he made open,
Bryngynge us lyfe agayne.

Thou only maker of all thynge,
Thou everlastynge lyght,
From ende to ende all rulynge,
By thyne own godly myght;
Turn thou our hartes unto thé;
And lyghten them with the veritie,
That they erre not from the ryght.

Let us increase in love of thè,
And in knowledge also;

G

That wee, believing stedfastlie,
May in spreit serue thee so;
That wee in heartes may sauour
Thy mercie and thy fauour,
And traist efter no mo.

Awake, O Lord, wee pray thee,
The Holie Ghost vs giue,
Whilke may our olde man mortifie,
That our new man may leiue.
So will we alwayes thanke thee,
That shawes vs so greit mercie,
And our sinnes does forgiue.*

That we belevynge stedfastly
May in spirite serve the so,
That we in our hartes may savoure
Thy mercy and thy favoure,
And to thryst after no mo.

Awake us, Lorde, we praye the;
Thy holy Spirite us geve,
Which maye our old man mortifie,
That our new man may lyve.
So wyll we alwaye thanke the,
That shewest us so great mercye,
And our synnes dost forgeve.

DEUS MISEREATUR.—Ps. lxvii.

O God be mercifull to vs,
And send to vs thy blessing;
Thy face shaw vs sa glorious,
And be euer to us luifing,
That men on eird may knaw thy way,
Thy sauing heill and righteousnes;
That they be noght led night nor day
Fra thy precepts, and trew justice,
To seik saluation quhair nane is.

Therefore the pepill might magnifie,
O God, all folke, and honour thy Name,
Let all pepill rejoyce gladlie,
Because thou dois right without blame.
The pepil does thou judge trewly,
And orders euery natioun :
Thou hes gouerned the eird justly
Euer sin the first creation,
Throw thy godly prouision.

God be mercyfull unto us,
And send over us his blessynge;
Shew us his presence glorious,
And be ever to us lovynge;
That men on earth may know thy way,
Thy savynge health and ryghteousnesse;
That they be not led by nyght nor day,
Throw the pretexte of trew justice
To seek salvacyon wher none is.

Therefore the people mought magnifie thee :
O God, let all folke honour thy name :
Let all the people rejoyce gladly,
Because thou dost ryght without blame.
The people dost thou judge truly,
And ord'rest every nacyon
Thou hast directe the earth justly,
Ever sense the first creacyon,
With thy godly provision.

* The authoress of the German hymn, of which these are translations, was Elizabeth Creutziger.
It was first published in 1524, and appeared in the Strassburg Hymn Book of 1537. It is partially translated by Miss Winkworth, in her " Chorale Book for England."

The pepil man spread thy name sa hie,
All pepill (O God) mon giue thee honor,
The eird alswa right plenteouslie
Mot encresse euer more and more,
And God, quhilk is our God ouer all,
Mot do vs gude and plesour,
God mot blesse vs great and small,
And all the warld him honour
Alway, for his might and power.

O God, let the people praise thee :
All people, God, mought give thee hon-
The earth also ryght plenteously   [oure ;
Mought increase ever more and more ;
And God which is our God over all,
Mought do us good and pleasure,
God blesse us now both great and small,
And all the world him honoure,
Fearynge alwaye his myght and power.*

MAGNIFICAT ANIMA MEA.

My saull does magnifie the Lord,
My spreit rejoyces greitumlie
In God my Sauiour, and in his word ;
For hee hes seene the law degree
Of mee his hand-maiden trewlie ;
Behald now, after this day
All generations sall speike of mee,
And call me blessed alway.

My soul doth magnifie the Lorde
My spret rejoyceth greitly
In God my Saviour and His worde :
For he hath sene the lowe degree
Of mee his handmayden truly.
Behold now after this day,
All generacyions shall speake of me
And call me blessed alwaye.

For hee that is onlie of might,
Hes done greit thinges vnto mee,
And halie is his name be right.
As for his endlesse mercie,
It endureth perpetuallie,
In euery generatioun,
And they that dreids him vnfenzeitlie,
Without dissimulatioun.   .

For he that is onely of myghte,
Hath done great thyngs for me ;
And holy is his name by ryght
As for his endless mercy,
It endureth perpetually,
In every generacyon,
On them that fear him unfaynedly,
Without dissimulacyon.

He shaws strenth with his arme potent,
Declares him selfe to bee of power ;
He scatters all men of proud intent,
Euen for their wickit behauiour,
Whilk reignes in their harts euery hour,
Hee puttes downe the mightie
From their hie estate and greit honour,
Extolling them of law degree.

He sheweth strength with his great arme,
Declaryng himselfe to be of power .
He scattereth the proud to their own harme,
Even with the wicked behavioure,
Of their own hertes every houre.
He putteth down the myghtye
From their hye seate and great honoure,
Exaltynge them of lowe degree.

* Luther's Hymn, which appear in the Enchiridion of 1524.

The hungrie hee feides with gude;
And lets the rich ga emptie,
When his owne people wants fude,
They think vpon his greit mercie,
And helpes his seruants ane and all,
Euen Israel hee hes promesit,
And to our fathers perpetuall,
Abraham and to his seid.

The hongrye fylleth he with good,
And letteth the ryche go emptie,
Where his owne people want no food :
He thynketh upon his mercye,
And helpeth his servant truely,
Even Israel as he promysed
Unto our fathers perpetually
Abraham and to his seed.*

NUNC DIMITTIS, THE PRAYER OF SYMEON, LUCK. II. CHAP.

PRESENTATION IN THE TEMPLE.

Lord, lat thy seruand now depart
  In gladnesse, rest, and peace :
I am rejoysit at my hert,
  To see his godly face,
Quhom faithfully thow promeist mee,
  Christ Jesus, King of grace.

In peace and joy I now depart,
  According to God's will,
For full of comfort is my heart,
  So calm and sweet and still ;
So doth God His promise keep,
And death to me is but a sleep.

.   .   .   .   .

Of Hethin folke blindit so soir,
  He is the verrie licht,
Quhilke neuer hard of him befoir,
  Nor saw him with their sicht.
He is the gloir, praise and decoir,
  And strenth of Israel richt.

.   .   .   .   .   .

He is the heathen's saving Light,
  And He will gently lead
Those who now know Thee not aright,
  And in His pastures feed ;
While His people's joy He is,
  Their sun, their glory, and their bliss.†

SALVUM ME FAC.—PSALM XI. [XII.]

(Wedderburn.)

(Miss Coxe's Translation of Luther's Hymn.)

Saif us gude Lord and succour send,
  For perishit is halynes,
And trewth away from men is wend,
  And fled fra them is faithfulness.

Look down, O Lord, from heaven behold,
  And let thy pity waken !
How few the flock within thy fold,
  Neglected and forsaken !

Translation of Polle's German hymn of 1524   † Do. of Luther's hymn of 1524.

Dissait amang them is sa sawin,
The verity may noght be knawin;
  Their toungs are full of feinzitnes.

Their lying toungs, O Lord, cut out,
  That speaks into thy contemptioun,
And sayis in all place round about,
  Our toungs hes ane exemptioun.
Even as we pleis our lips may lie,
For we have all authority,
  Nane hes of us dominion.

But God hes said, and will it keip,
  I will rise up incontinent,
For the opprest that sair dois weip,
  And murning of the indigent.
The poor that vexit is so sore,
I will them save and them restore
  Fra wicked toung's teichment.

Almost thou'lt seek for faith in vain,
And those who should thy truth maintain,
  Thy word from us have taken.

God surely will uproot all those
  With vain deceits who store us,
With haughty tongue who God oppose,
  And say, "Who'll stand before us?
By right or might we will prevail,
What we determine cannot fail,
  For who can lord it o'er us?"

For this, saith God, I will arise,
  These wolves my flock are rending:
I've heard my people's bitter sighs
  To heaven my throne ascending:
Now will I up and set at rest
Each weary soul by fraud opprest,
  The poor with might defending.

Preserve us, Lord, by thy dere word,
From Turke and Pope defend us, Lord,
Which both would thrust out of his throne
Our Lord Jesus Christ thy deare Sone. ·

Lord, keep us by thy word in hope,
And check the murder of Turk and Pope,
Who Jesus Christ thine only Son
Fain would tumble from his throne.†

II.

THE LORD'S PRAYER.

(From Knox's Psalter.)

DAS VATER UNSER.

Our Father which in heaven art,
  And makes us all one brotherhood:
Wee call upon thee with our heart,
  Our heavenly Father and our God:
Grant wee pray not with lips alone,
But with the hearts deep sigh and grone.

Vater unser im himmelreich,
  der du uns alle heissest gleich
Brüder sein und dich rufen an,
  und wilt das beten von uns han:
Gib dass nicht bet allein der mund,
  hilf dass es geh von hertzen grund.

* From old Scotch MS. music-book.

† M'Donnell's translation of Luther's hymn.

Thy blessed Name bee sanctified,
  Thine holy Word mought us inflame :
In holy life for to abide,
  To magnifie thine holy Name :
From all errours defend and keep
The little flock of thy poor sheep.

Thy kingdome come even at this houre
  And henceforth everlastingly ;
Thine Holy Ghost into us powre,
  With all his gifts most plenteously ;
From Sathan's rage and filthy band
Defend us with thy mighty hand,

Thy will be done with diligence,
  Like as in heaven in earth also :
In trouble grant us patience,
  Thee to obey in wealth and wo :
Let not flesh, blood, nor any ill
Prevaile against Thine holy will.

Give us this day our dayly bread,
  And all other good gifts of thine :
Keep us from war, and from bloodshed,
  Also from sicknesse, dearth and pine :
That we may live in quyetnesse,
Without all greedie carefulnesse,

Forgive us our offences all,
  Relieve our careful conscience :
As we forgive both great and small
  Who unto us have done offence :
Prepare us, Lord, for to serve thee
In perfect love and unitie.

O Lord, into temptation
  Lead us not when the fiend doth rage,
To withstand his invasion
  Give power and strength to every age.
Arme and make strong thy feeble host
With faith, and with the Holy Ghost.

Geheiliget werd der name dein,
  dein wort bei uns hilf halten rein,
Dass auch wir leben heiliglich,
  nach deinem namen würdiglich.
Herr behüt uns für falscher lehr,
  das arm verfüret volk bekehr.

Es komm dein reich zu diser zeit,
  und dort hernach in ewigkeit,
Der heilig Geist uns wohne bei
  mit seinem gaben mancherlei,
Des Satan's zorn und gross gewalt
  zerbrich, für ihm dein kirch erhalt.

Dein will gescheh, Herr Gott, zugleich
  auf erden wie im himmelreich,
Gib uns geduld in leidenszeit,
  gehorsam sein in lieb und leid,
Wehr und steur allem fleisch und blut,
  das wider deinen willen thut.

Gib uns heut unser täglich brot,
  und was mann darf zur leibes noth,
Behüt uns Herr für unfried und streit,
  fur zeuchen und fur theur zeit,
Dass wir in guten frieden stehn,
  der sorg und geizes mussig gehn.

All unser schuld vergib uns, Herr,
  dass sie uns nicht betrüben mehr,
Wie wir auch unsern schuldigern
  ihr schuld und fehl vergeben gern.
Zu dienen mach uns all bereit,
  in rechter lieb und einnigkeit.

Fuhr uns, Herr, in versuchung nicht,
  wenn uns der böse geist anficht,
Zur linken und zur rechten hand,
  hilf uns thun starken widerstand,
Im glauben fest und wohl gerust,
  und durch den heilgen Geistes trost.

O Lord, from evil delyver us,
   The days and times are dangerous :
From everlasting death save us,
   And in our last end comfort us :
A blessed end to us bequeath,
Into thine hands our soules receive.

For thou, O Lord, art King of kings,
   And thou hast power over all :
Thy glory shyneth in all things,
   In the wide world universall :
Amen, let it be done, O Lord,
That we have praid with one accord.

Von allen ubel uns erlös,
   es sind die zeit und tage bös,
Erlös uns vom ewigen tod,
   und tröst uns in der letzten noth,
Bescher uns auch ein seligs end,
   nimm unser seel in deinem händ.

Amen, das ist, es werde wahr.
   Stark unsern glauben immerdar,
Auf dass wir ia nicht zweifeln d'ran.
   das wir hiemet, gebeten ha'n,
Auf dein wort in dem namen dein,
   so sprechen wir das Amen fein.

III.

THE EFFECT OF THE SACRAMENT OF
   BAPTISME, AND FIRST INSTITUTION
   THAIROF, DECLAIRING ALSWA QUHAT
   SINGULAR COMFORT WE OBTEINE BE
   THE SAMING.

EIN GEISTLICH LIED VON UNSRER HEILI-
   GEN TAUFE, DARIN FEIN KURTZ GEFAS-
   SET, WAS SIE SEY, WER SIE GESTIFFTET
   HABE, WAS SIE NUTZE, &c.

Christ baptist was be John in Jordan flude,
For to fulfill for vs all richteousnes,
And our baptisme dotit with sanctitude,
And greit vertew, to wesche our sinfulnes,
To drowne the deid, and hell for to op-
   pres,   [be,
Quhen Goddis word, with water joynit
Throw faith to giue vs lyfe eternally.

For our waiknes God of his mercy sweit,
To strenth our faith ordan'd this Sacrament,
In name of Father, Sone, and Haly Spreit,

Christ unser Herr zum Jordan kam
   nach seines Vaters willen,
Von sanct Johanns die taufe nahm,
   sein werk und amt zu'rfüllen.
     Da wollt er stiften uns ein bad,
   zu waschen uns von sünden,
ersaufen auch den bittern tod
   durch sein selbs blut und wunden,
   es galt ein neues Leben.

So hört und merket alle wohl,
   was Gott heisst selbs die taufe
Und was ein Christen glauben soll,

To wesche our body, and in our mynde
   to prent
That word and water outward represent,
Throw working of the Spreit into our
   hart,   [sin inwart.
That Christis blude weschis away the
   .   .   .   .   .

Be figure and be worde, Christ did vs
   teich,   [cleir,
The Fatheris voice was hard saying full
Jesus, quhome I haif send my word to
   preich,
He is my well-belouit Sone so deir,
In word, in wark, allone ze sall him heir,
In him is all my plesour and delite,
To him I you commit baith small and greit.

The Haly Gaist come doun to testifie,
His doctrine and his baptisme to declair,
In forme of dow sat on him soberlie,
In our baptisme to dout not nor despair,
Baith Father, Sone, and Haly Gaist, ar
   thair
To be our gyde, the Trynitie him sell
Hes geuin in eird with vs to dwell.

Christ bad his apostillis preich to all
   creature,   [lorne;
That they with sin and hell war all for-
Quha will beleif and traist my wordis sure,
And baptist is, and now againe is borne,
And Sathan and his warkis hes forsworne,
Thay salbe saif, and neuer mair sall die,
Bot ring in glorie perpetuall with me.

Quha will not this greit grace beleif, to
   hell
Salbe condempnit with eternall deid,
Quhair purgatorie and pardonis will not sell

zu meiden ketzerhaufen :   [sei
   Gott spricht und will, das wasser
   doch nicht allein schlecht wasser,
sein heiligs wort ist auch dabei
mit reichem geist ohn massen,
der ist allhie der taufer.

Solchs hat er uns beweiset klar
   mit bilden und mit worten ;
Des vaters stimm man offenbar
   daselbs am Jordan hörte,
      Er sprach : Das ist mein lieber Son,
   an dem ich hab gefallen,
den will ich euch befohlen han,
   dass ihr ihn horet alle,
   und folget seinen leren.

Auch Gottes Sohn hie selber steht
   in seiner zarten menschheit,
Der heilig geist hernider fährt
   in taubenbild verkleidet,
      Dass wir nicht sollen zweifeln d'ran,
   wenn wir getaufet werden
all drei person getaufet han,
   damit bei uns auf erden
   zu wohnen sich ergeben.

Sein jünger heisst der Herre Christ :
   geht hin, all welt zu lehren,
Dass sie verlor'n in sünden ist,
   sich soll zur busse kehren
      Wer glaubet und sich taufen lässt,
   soll dadurch selig werden,
ein neugeborner mensch er heisst,
   der nicht mehr könne sterben,
   das himmelreich soll erben.

Wer nicht glaubt diser grossen gnad,
   der bleibt in seinen sunden,
Und ist verdammt zum ewigen tod
   tief in der höllen grunde.

And gud intent thair pylat plycht and
  leid.
Dum ceremoneis, the quhilk them self
  hes maid,   [keip,
And wowis vaine, quhilk thay did neuer
Sall gar them gnasche thair teith, and
  eyis weip.

Our eine seis outward bot the watter
  cauld,
Bot our pure faith the power spirituall
Of Christis blude inwart it dois behald,
Quhilk is ane leuand well celestiall,
Zit for to purge the penetant withall.
Our nature sin in Adam to expell,
And all trespas committit be our sell.

 . . . .

Nichts hilft sein eigen heiligkeit,
  all sein thun ist verloren,
die erbsund machts zur nichtigkeit,
  darin er ist geboren,
  vermag ihm selbs nicht z'helfen.

Das aug allein das wasser sieht,
  wie menschen wasser giessen,
Der glaub im geist die kraft versteht
  des blutes Jesu Christi,
    Und ist fur ihm ein rothe fluth,
  von Christus blut gefarbet,
die allen schaden heilen thut
  von Adam her geerbet,
auch von uns selbs begangen.

THE SUPPER OF THE LORD, AND RICHT
USE OF IT.†

To be Sung.

DAS LIED JOHANNIS HUSSEN "JESUS
CHRISTUS NOSTRA SALUS."—*Gebessert.*

Our Saviour Christ, king of grace,
With God the Father made our peace,
And with his bludie wounds feill,
Hes us redemit from the hell.

And he that we sould not forget,
Gaif us his body for to eit,
In forme of breid, and gaue us syne
His blude to drink, in forme of wyne.

Quha will ressave this sacrament,
Suld have trew faith, and sin repent ;
Quha usis it unworthlie
Ressavis deid eternallie.

Jesus Christus, unser Heiland,
der von uns den Gottes zorn wand,
Durch das bitter leiden sein
half er uns aus der hellen pein.

Dass wir nimmer des vergessen,
gab er uns sein leib zu essen,
Verborgen im brot so klein,
und zu trinken sein blut im wein.

Wer sich will zu dem tisch machen,
der hab wol acht auf sein sachen ;
Wer unwürdig hinzu geht
für das leben den todt empfeht.

---

* Luther is the author of this hymn. It was published in 1541, and appears in the Strassburg book
of 1545.
  † The German is by Luther from a Latin hymn of Huss. It also is found in the Strassburg Hymn-
book of 1545.

We suld to God give prais and gloir,   Du sollt Gott den vater preisen
That sched his blude us to restoir ;   dass er dich so wol wollt speisen
Eit this in his remembrance,   Und für deine missethat
In signe of thy deliverance.   in den todt sein Sohn geben hat.

Thow sould not dout, but fast beleve,   Du sollt glauben und nicht wanken,
That Christis body sall resave   dass ein speise sei den kranken,
All them that in heaviness   Den ihr herz von sünden schwer :
Repentand for thair sinfulnes.   und für angst ist betrübet sehr.

Sik grace and mercie nane can traist,   Solch gross gnad und barmherzigkeit
Bot thay that troublit hertis haist.   Sucht ein herz in grosser arbeit:
Feill thow than sin, and abstene thy sell,   Ist dir wohl, so bleib davon,
Or thy reward salbe in hell.   dass du nicht kriegest bösen lohn.

Christ sayis, Sinneris, cum unto me,   Er spricht selber : kommt ihr armen,
Quhilk mester hes of my mercie.   lasst mich über euch erbarmen :
Neidis thow not my medecine,   Kein arzt ist dem starken noth,
I lose my paine and travelling.   sein kunst wird an ihm gar ein spott.

Give thow thy self thy saull culd win,   Hättst du dir was könnt erwerben,
In vaine I diet for thy sinne ;   was dürft ich denn für dich sterben?
My supper is not greithit for thee,   Dieser tisch auch dir nicht gilt,
Give thow can make thy self supplé.   so du selber dir helfen willt.

Will thow thy sinfull lyfe confesse,   Glaubst du das von herzen grunde
And with this wark thy faith expres,   und bekennest mit dem munde,
Sa are ye worthie, small and greit,   So bist du recht wol geschickt
And it sall strenth your faith perfyte.   und die speise dein seel erquickt.

And thow sall thankfull be thairfor,   Die frucht soll auch nicht aus bleiben.
And loue thy God for euermoir ;   deinen nächsten sollt du lieben,
Thy nichbour lufe, and als supplé   Dass er dein geniessen kann,
His neid, as Christ has done for thé.   wie dein Gott an dir hat gethan.

Ane grace to be sung.

We thank thee, Lord, of thy gudnes,
  Throw Jesus Christ our gratious Lord,
For thy grit mercy and gentilnes
  Quhilk feidis us with thy sweit word;
Sen all that ever tuk life of thee,
Thow satisfyis abundantlie,
  We praise thee all with one accord.

As thow hes fed the sinfull fleshe,
  Quhilk sone sall die and turn in ash,
Siclyke the sillie saul refreshe,
  The quhilk immortal creat was.
God, for thy grace and mercy greit,
Grant us ane stedfast faith perfyte,
  And in thy glory with thee to passe.

To God on hicht be loving maist,
  Quhilk loussis sin alanerlie,
Till all that will repent and traist
  On Jesus Christ his Sone onlie:
Thow makis them thy sone and heir,
Throw him thow will them saif from cair,
  To whom be gloir eternallie.

Ein lobgesang nach dem essen.

O Gott wir danken deiner güt
  durch Christum unsern Herren
Für deine wohlthat uberschütt,
  der du uns thust ernehren.
All's was den athem ie gewan
hast du sein noth durfft lassen ha'n
  dir gescheh lob und auch ehre.

Als du nun Herr gespeiset hast
  den leichnam der verdirbet
So lass die seel auch seyn dein gast,
  die durch dir nimmer stirbet,
Dein heilsam wort ihr speise sey
bis sie auch endlich wird gantz frei
  unds himmelreich ererben.

Lob, ehr und dank zu aller zeit
  Sey dir Vat'r in der höhe :
Der du der sund uns machest quit,
  durch einen festen glauben,
An demem eingebornen Sohn,
auf dass wir mit ihm kinder seyn,
  dich ewig preisen, Amen.[*]

ANE SANG OF OUR CORRUPT NATURE : AND THE ONLY REMEID THAIROF.

VON DER SUNDE, &c.

We wratchit sinners pure,
  Our sin hes vs forlorne,
Thairin all creature consauit is and borne.
  Sin hes wrocht vs sic paine,
  That we, without remeid,
Condamnit are and slaine to hell, the
  deuill, and deid.   [mercy, &c.
Lord haue mercie on vs. Christ haue

O wir armen Sünder
  Unser missethat
Darin wir empfangen und geboren sind,
  Hat gebracht uns alle
  In solche grosse noth,
Dass wir unterworfen sind dem ewigen
  todt,   [Eleison.
Kyrie Eleison, Christe Eleison, Kyrie

---

[*] Nicolas Bon is said to be the author. The Hymn appears in the Magdeburg book of 1545.

Our warkis can not be
As dois the law requyre,
Nor yet can satisfie our Fatheris wrath
and ire,
No deid can mak vs fre
From our grit sinfulnes,
But Goddis Sone must die, for our vn-
richteousnes.
Lord haue mercy, Christ haue, &c.

Aus dem todt wir kondten
Durch unser eigen werk,
Nimmer werden gereuet, die sünde war
zu starck.
Dass wir würden erloset,
So kont's nicht anders seyn
Den Gottes Sohn muss leiden des Todes
bitter pein.
Kyrie, Eleison, Christe Eleison, Kyrie
Eleison.

Or had not Christ bene send,
    Cled in our vylde nature,
Fra hell vs to defend,
    Our deidlie wound to cure,
And willinglie to die,
    Fra sin to mak vs cleane,
We had eternally
    In hell condampnit bene.
Lord haue mercy, Christ haue mercie,
    Lord, &c.

So nicht wär' gekommen
Christus in die welt,
Und hätt an sich genommen
Unser arme gestalt,
Und für die Sünde
Gestorben williglich
So hätten wir müssen
Verdampt seyn ewiglich
Kyrie Eleison, Christe Elison, Kyrie
Eleison.

Man now hes thy peace,
    Sik lufe God schawit thé:
He takis the in his grace,
    His mortall enemie,
Throw faith in Chryst so kynde,
    Quhilk frelie gaue him sell
On croce for to be pynd,
    To saif vs from the hell.
Lord haue mercy, Christ haue mercie,
    Lord, &c.

Solche grosse gnade
Und väterliche gunst,
Hat uns Gott erzeiget
Lauter gar umsonst
In Christo seinem Sohne
Der sich gegeben hat
In den todt des kreutzes
Zu unser seligkeit,
Kyrie Eleison, Christe Eleison, Kyrie.
Eleison.

This we sould euer beleue,
    And nocht despair for sin,
For hell can not vs greue,
    The deid nor devill thairin
We ar maid just and richt,

Des sollen wir uns trösten
Gegen sünd und todt,
Und nicht verzagen
Fur der hellen Glut
Denn wir sind gerettet

And fréed from panes sore,
Throw Christ, that Lord of micht,
  Blissit for euermore.
Lord haue mercie, Christ haue mercie,
  Lord, &c.

Aus aller fährligkeit
Durch Christum unsern Herren
  Gebenedeyt in ewigkeit
Kyrie Eleison, Christe Eleison, Kyrie
  Eleison.

Thairfoir lat vs loue and praise
  God the Father feruentlie.
We thank ane thousand syse
  His Sonnis maiestie.
We pray the Haly Gaist
  Our sin to mortifye,
And nocht despair, bot traist
  Goddis word maist faithfully.
Lord haue mercy, Christ haue mercy,
  Lord, &c.

Darum woll'n wir loben
Und danken allezeit
Den Vater und dem Sohne
Und dem Heiligen Geist,
Und bitten dass sie wollen
Behüten uns für gefahr
Und dass wir stets bleiben
Bey seinem heiligen wort.
Kyrie Eleison, Christe Eleison, Kyrie
  Eleison.

ANE SANG OF THE FLESCHE AND THE SPIRIT.

VON DEM STREITE DES FLEYSCHES WIDER DEN GEIST.

All Christen men take tent and lier,
How saull and body ar at wier,
Upon this eird baith lait and eir,
With cruell battell identlie,
And ane may nocht ane vther flie.

Nun horend zu, ihr Christen leut,
wie leyb vnd seel gegnander streyt :
  Allhie auff erd in diser zeyt
heb'n sie ein stettigs kriegen,
keins mag vom andern fliehen.

The Flesche.

The Flesche said, Sen I haif haill,
I will in zouth with lustis daill,
Or age with sorrow me assail ;
With ioy I will my time ouerdryue,
And will not with my lustis stryue.

Der leyb der spricht, Ich bin gesundt,
ich hab noch vil der guten stundt :
  Ehe mir das traurig alter kompt
will ich in freuden leben,
nach leyblich'n lusten streben.

---

* This Hymn is said to be by Hermann Bonn, and appears in the Magdeburg Hymn book of 1543.

The Spirit.

The Spreit said, Thocht I charge thé nocht,
Dreid God, and haue his law in thocht,
Thow hecht quhen thow to font was
Efter his law lust to refraine,   [brocht,
And nocht to wirk his word agane.

Die seele spricht, Ich radt dirs nicht!
Ach, forchst du nicht Gott's strengs gericht?
Du hast dich in der tauff verpflicht,
nach Gottes will'n zu leben,
sei'm wort nicht wider streben.

The Flesche.

The Flesche said, I am stark and wycht
To wacht gude wyne, fresche, cauld and
        bricht,
And tak my plesour day and nicht,
With singing, playing, and to dance,
And set on sax and sevin the chance.

Der leyb spricht, Ich bin stoltz vnd fein
mit guten g'sellen beim kulen wein,
Da will ich frisch und frölich sein
mit singen springen tantzen,
wils wagen auff die schantzen !

The Spirit.

The Spirit said, Think on the rich man,
Quhilk all tyme in his lustis ran,
Body and saull he loissit than,
And synde was buryit into hell,
As Jesus Christ hes said him sell.

Die seele spricht, Denck an Reichen man,
der sich nahm zeitlichs wollust an!
Der muss mit leyb vnd seel davon,
ward in die hell begraben,
als Christus selb thut sagen.

The Flesche.

The Flesche said, Quhat hald I of this,
Laser yneuch and tyme thair is
In age for till amend my misse,
And from my vicious lyfe conuert,
Quhen sadnes hes ouer set my hart.

Der leyb spricht, Was acht ich der sag !
ich hab' vor mir noch manchen tag,
Darinn ich mich wohl bessern mag,
vnd mich von sunden kehren,
wenn sich mein traur'n thut mehren.

The Spirit.

The Spirit said, Power thow hes none,
In youcht nor zit in eild bygone.
With twinkling of ane eye anone,
God sall thé tak at euin or morne,
No certayne tyme set thé beforne.

Die seel spricht, Du hast dein kein g'walt,
du seyest g'leich jung oder alt,
Gott hat dich in ei'm augenblick gefalt,
den abend und den morgen,
die stund ist dir verborgen.

The Flesche.

The Flesche said, All tyme air and lait,
I see all warldly wyse estait
Hald lust vertew in thair consait,
With them I will persew my weird,
Als long as I leue on this eird.

Der leyb spricht, Es sey früh oder spat,
ch siehe vor mir die weltlich rott,
Ein yeder tracht nach zeitlichem rath :
darnach will ich auch streben,
die weyl ich hab das leben.

The Spirit.

The Spirit, Zit sall cum the day
The saull sall part the body fray;
Than quhat sall help thy game or play
Quhen thow man turnit be in as
At first in eird quhen thow maide was.

Die seel spricht es kompt die zeyt,
das leyb vnd seel von ander scheydt :
Was hilfft dich dann dein grosser geytz
du must zu Aschen werden,
dann du bist gemacht aus erden.

The Flesche.

The Flesche said, Thow hes vincust me,
I traist eternall gloir to se,
Christ grant that I may cum thairby,
Now will I to my God returne,
Repent my sin richt sore I murn.

Der leyb der spricht, Du machst mir bang,
erst mich nach ewiger freud verlangt !
Christus helff mir zum anfang,
das mich zum vat'r bekehren
mein trauren will sich mehren.

The Spirit.

The Spirit, Nane to schame I dryue,
Ane contreit hert help God alyue,
The flesche man die with pane and stryue,
For it was borne to that intent,
In eird with wormes for to be rent.

Die seel die spricht, Ich treyb kein schertz :
Gott fordert ein zerknirschtes hertz !
Der leyb muss hie absterben durch
dann er ist zeytlich geboren [schmertz,
den würmen ausserkohren.

The Flesche.

The flesche said, O Lord God of peace,
Help me to turne throw Christis grace,
O Holy Ghost my faith incresse,
That I may thole this eirthlie noy,
My hope is in eternall joy.

Der leyb der spricht, O Gott, mein herr,
hilff das ich mich durch Christum b'kehr !
O heyliger Geyst, mein glauben mehr '
Hilff mirs zeytlich erleyden,
mich tröst in ewiger freuden !

The Spirit.

The Spirit said, Now I haif my micht,
Thoch I be ane vnworthie knycht.
Thow God the quhilk is onlie richt,
Thow saif me from the deuillis net:
Thairfore thow on the croce was plet.

Die seel spricht, nun hab ich recht,
wiewohl ich bin ein unnütz knecht
  O Gott, du bist allein gerecht.
Löss mich von's teuffels banden,
d'rumb du am Creutz bist g'hangen.

The Dyter.

Now hes this ballat heir an end,
God grant ilk man his hart a kend,
To sin na more, syne to Christ wend.
Than sall he turne agane to vs,
And giue vs his eternall blys.

Also hat dises lied ein endt.
Gott woll das yeder sein hertz erkendt
  Vnd sich von sünden zu Christo wendt;
so würd er zu vns kehren,
die ewig freud bescheren.*

ANE SANG OF THE CROCE, AND THE
FRUTE THAIROF.

EIN GEISTLICH LIED *von dem XIten
Capitel Matthei.*

Cum heir, sayis Goddis Sonne to me,
Sinners that heuie laden be,
  I will zour sillie saull refresche.
Cum zoung and auld baith man and wife,
I will zow gif eternall life,   [flesche.
  Thocht trowblit heir sore be zour

Kompt her zu mir, spricht Gottes Sohn,
all die ihr seid beschweret nun,
  mit sunden hart beladen,
Ihr jungen, alt, frauen vnd mann!
ich will euch geben, was ich ha'n,
  wil heilen euren schaden.

My zok is sweit, my burding small,
Quha drawis efter me, they sall
  Eschaip eternall deid and fire;
For I sall help them in thair draucht,
That they sall cum, as I haue taucht,
  To gloir and joy, and heuin impire.

Mein joch ist süss, mein bürd gering,
wer mir's nachträgt in dem geding,
  der hell wird er entweichen,
Ich wil ihm trewlich helffen tragen,
mit meiner hülff wird ers erjagen
  das ewig himmelreiche.

Quhat I haue teichit lait and air,
Quhat I haif tholit les and mair,

Was ich g'than hab vnd gelitten hie
in meinem leben spat vnd früh,

---

* This hymn is by John Witzstadt von Wirtheim. It does not appear in the Strassburg Hymn
Books, but is found in the Magdeburg book of 1541.

That preis zou euer to fulfill;
And thocht zour flesche be heir opprest,
Zit all thing wirk sall for the best;
   For sa is richt, and Goddis will.

das sollt ihr auch erfüllen.
Was ihr gedenkt, ja redt und thut,
das wird euch alles recht und gut,
   wenn's g'schieht nach Gottes willen.

The warld wald sauit be, and faine
Wald cum to gloir bot croce or paine,
   Quhilk Christis flock must suffer heir.
Bot paine thair is na vther way
To cum to gloir, and put away
   Eternall hellis paine, bot peir.

Gern wollt die welt auch selig sein,
wenn nur nicht war die schwere pein,
   die alle Christen leiden :
So mag es anders nicht gesein,
darum ergib dich nur darein,
   wer ewig pein will meiden !

That the faithfull must the croce indure,
Witnes beiris all creature,
   Subdewit vnto vanitie,
Quha will not thole in Christis name,
The deuill sall wirk him sik ane schame,
   With peirles paine perpetuallie.

All creatur bezeugen das,
was lebt in wasser, laub vnd gras :
   sein leiden kann er nicht meiden.
Wer denn in Gottes nam nicht will,
zu letzt muss er des Teuffels ziel
   mit schwerem g'wissen leiden.

To day ane man is fresche and fair,
To morne he lyis sick and sair,
   Syne dulefullie domet to deid.
Euin like as in the feild ane floure,
The day is sweit, the morne is sour ;
   So all this wretchit warld sall feade.

Heut ist der mensch schön, jung vnd lang,
sieh, morgen ist er schwach vnd krank,
   bald muss er auch gar sterben :
Gleich wie die blumen auff dem feld,
also wird auch die schone welt
   in einem huy verderben.

The godles dreidis sair to die,
But quhen he can no farther flie,
   And faine his sinfull lyfe wald mend,
They grip sa fast his geir to get,
The sillie saull is quyte forzet,
   Quhill haistelie gais out his end.

Die welt erzittert ob dem tod,
wenn ein'r liegt in der letzten noth,
   denn will er g'leich fromm werden :
Einer schafft diess, der ander das,
sein'r armen seel er gantz vergass,
   dieweil er lebt auff erden.

Quhen he persauis na remeid,
Than greuously he gais to deid,
   And grugeand geuis vp the gaist.
Sair I suspect God accuse,
His sectouris and himself refuse,
   Than sa vnthankfullie deceist.

Vnd wenn er nimmer leben mag,
so hebt er an ein grosse klag.
   will sich erst Gott ergeben :
Ich fürcht fürwar, die Gottlich gnad,
die er allzeit verspottet hat,
   werd schwerlich ob ihm schweben.

I

The rich man helpis not his gude,   Dem reichen hilfft doch nicht sein gut,
The nobill nocht his royall blude;   dem jungen nicht sein stoltzer muth,
   For thay sall baith thair querrell tyne;   er muss aus diesem meyen :
Thocht ane had all this warld so wyde,   Wenn einer hätt die gantze welt,
Zit he sall die with dule and pyne,   silber vnd gold vnd alles geld,
   With gold and precious stones of pryde.   noch muss er an den reihen.

Knawledge concernis not the clerk,   Dem gelehrten hilfft doch nicht sein kunst,
Nor hypocreit his haly wark;   die weltlich pracht ist gar vmsonst,
   Bot thay but dout with deid man dwell.   wir müssen alle sterben :
Quha will not baill to Christ him giue,   Wer sich in Christo nicht ergeit,
Quhill in this present lyfe he liue,   weil er lebet in gnaden zeit,
   For euer mair sall die in hell.   ewig muss er verderben.

Mark weill thairfoir, my sonnis sweit,   Höret vnd merckt, ihr lieben kind,
How Christis croce is for zou meit.   die jetzund Gott ergeben sind,
   O moue zou not in mynde thairfoir,   lasst euch die müh nicht reuen;
Bot at his word stand stedfastlie,   Halt't stets am heiligen Gottes wort,
And with him suffer pacientlie,   das ist euer trost und höchster hort,
   Giue ze waid enter in his gloir.   Gott wird euch schon erfreuen.

Do gude for euill, and leid zour lyfe   Schaut, dass ihr gut's um übel's gebt,
Without reprufe, but pryde or stryfe,   schaut, dass ihr hie unschuldig lebt,
   And thole the warldis wraith to rage.   lasst euch die welt nicht äffen :
O enter be that narrow rode;   Gebt Gott die rach und alle ehr,
Gif gloir and vengence vnto God,   den engen steig geht immer her,
   And he thair cruell ire sall swaye.   Gott wird die welt schon straffen.

Quhen that zour flesche hes all the will, Wenn es euch gieng nach fleisches muth,
And may zour lustis all fulfill,   in gunst und g'sund mit grossem gut,
   Ze are but dout the feindis pray.   würdt ihr gar bald erkalten :
God sendis you the croce thairfor,   Darum schickt Gott die trübsal her,
To mortifie zour flesche thairfor,   damit euer fleisch gezüchtigt werd,
   To saif your sillie saull for ay.   Zu ewig freud erhalten.

And quhen this schort pyne do you greif, Ist euch das creutz bitter vnd schwer :
Then think on hell the lang mischief,   gedenkt, wie heiss die helle wär,
   Quhair mony ane for ay sall murne,   darin die welt thut rennen,

And saull and bodie sall remaine,
For euer mair with cruell paine,
  Endless for ay, without returne.

Bot he sall, after warldlie pyne,
Rejoyce with Christ withouttin syne,
  Quhair na myndis memoriall
Can think, nor toung can tell the tryne,
Nor haif the gloir quhilk sall propyne
  That michtie Lord vnto vs all.

For quhat eternall God of peace
Hes promeist, throw his Spirit of grace,
  And syne sworn be his holie name,
That he sall hauld baith trew and sune.
God grant that we may se his throne,
  Throw faith in Jesus Christ.   Amen.

Mit leib vnd seel muss leiden sein
ohn unterlass die ewig pein
  vnd mag doch nicht verbrennen!

Ihr aber werdt nach dieser zeit
mit Christo haben ewig freud,
  dahin sollt ihr gedenken.
Es lebt kein mann der's aussprechen kann
die glori und den ewigen lohn,
  den euch der Herr wird schenken!

Vnd was der ewig gütig Gott
in seinem geist versprochen hat,
  geschworen bey seinem namen,
Das hält und gibt er g'wiss fürwahr:
der helff uns an der engel schaar
  durch Jesum Christum, Amen!*

PRINCIPALL POINTES OF THE PASSIOUN,
SCHORTLIE CORRECTIT.

GESANG VOM WORTE
GOTTES.

Helpe, God, the former of all thing,
  That to thy gloir may bee my dyte:
Be baith at end and beginning,
  That I may make my sang perfyte,
Of Jesus Christes passioun,
Sinnaris onely saluatioun,
  As witnesse is thy word in write.

Thy word for euer sall remaine,
  As in his buke wrytes Esay,
Baith heuin and eird sall turne againe,
  Or thy trew word cum to decay.

Hilff, Gott, dass mir gelinge,
  du edler schöpffer mein,
Die silben reimen zwingen
  zu lob den ehren dein!
  Dass ich mag frolich heben an
von deinem wort zu singen,
Herr, du wollest mir beystahn!

Ewig dein wort thut bleiben,
  wie Esaias meldt;
In seinem buch thut schreiben:
  ehe wird vergehn die welt

---

* This Hymn is ascribed to John Witzstadt von Wertheim. It is said to have appeared in 1536, and is found in a Strassburg hymn-book of 1544.

Thou cannot like ane man repent,
  To change thy purpose or intent,
  Bot steidfast is thy word for ay.

Und was Gott selber je beschuff,
  Solt es alles verderben,
  er thät kein wiederruff.

Jesus, the Father's Word alone,
  Discendit in an Virgine pure,
With meruellis greit and mony one ;
  And be Judas that fals tratour,
That Lambe for sober summe was sauld,
And gaif his lyfe, for cause hee wald
  Redeme all sinfull creature.

Jesus das wort des Vaters,
  ist kommen in die welt
Mit grossen wunderthaten,
  verkaufft um schnodes geld
  Durch Judam, seiner Jünger ein
ward er in tod gegeben,
  Jesus, das lämmelein.

When eitin was the Paschall Lambe,
  Christ tuke the breid his handis within,
Blyssing it, brake it, gaif the sume
  Till his apostles mair and min,
Eit that, for my body is this,
Quhilk for your sakis geuin is,
  Intill remissioun of your sin.

Nachdem sie hatten gessen,
vernembt, das Osterlamb,
  Da thät er nicht vergessen,
  das brod in seine hand nahm,
  Sprach : esset, das ist mein leichnam
der fur euch wird gegeben   [lind,
  Zur vergebung euer sünd.

Siclyke hee gaif them for to drinke
  In wyne his blude the quhilke was sched,
Upon his precious deid to thinke,
  On him remembrance to be made.
Quha eitis this blissit sacrament,
Worthelie with trew intent
  Sall neuer see eternall deid.

Reicht ihn auch dar zu trincken
In wein sein blut so roth :
  Sein tod sollt ihr verkünden,
  Paulus beschrieben hat :
  Wer würdig isst von diesem brod
und trincket von dem kelche,
  wird nicht sehen den tod.

Jesus wusche his apostlis feit,
  Schawand exempil of lowlynesse,
And chargit them with wordis sweit,
  That lufe amang them suld incres.
For thairby suld it cum to licht,
That ye are my disciplis richt,
  Gif ye amang you lufe possesse.

Jesus wusch ihn ihr fusse
  wohl zu derselben stund,
Lehret sie mit worten süsse
  aus seinem Göttlichen mund ;
  Liebet einander alle zeit,
dabey wird man erkennen
  das ihr mein Jünger seid.

Efter this prayer passit he,
  And met the Jewis quhilk him socht ;

Christus der Herr im garten,
da er gebetet hat,

When they had bound him cruellie,
  Before the judges they him brocht.
First they him scurgit, and for scorne
Him crownit with ane crowne of thorne,
  Syne dampnit him to deid for nocht.

Der Jüden thät er warten,
von ihn gebunden hart,
  Sie führten ihn zum richter dar,
gegeisselt und gekrönet,
zum tod verurtheilt ward.

That Prince on croce they lift on hicht,
  For our redemptioun that thocht lang;
Hee said, I thirst with all my micht
  To saif mankynde fra painis strang.
Hee that all warldis was beforne,
Came doun of Marie to be borne,
  For our trespasse on croce hee hang.

Hoch an ein creutz gehangen,
der hoch geborne Fürst,
Nach uns thät ihn verlangen,
darum sprach er: mich dürst!
  Vernimm; nach unser seligkeit,
darum ein mensch geboren
von einer reinen magd.

Then hee his heid culd incline,
  As wryttis John, and gaif the gaist.
And off the croce tane was syne,
  And laid in grave; but soone in haist,
Leuand, he rais on the thrid day,
And to his apostles did say,
  To them appeirand maist and leist.

Mit seinem haupt geneiget
er seinen geist aufgab,
Als uns Johannes zeiget,
er ward genommen ab
  Vom creutz, ins grab ward er gelegt,
am dritten tag erstanden,
wie er vor hat gesagt.

And syne he did his apostillis teiche,
  Throw all the warlde for to passe,
And tell all creature for to preich,
  As they of him instructit was :
Quha baptist is, and will beleeue,
Eternall deid sall not them greeue,
  Bot salbe sauit mair and lesse.

Und in den selben tagen
Jesus sein Jünger lehrt,
Allein sein wort zu tragen,
predigen in aller welt :
  Wer glauben thut und wird getaufft,
der hat das ewig leben,
ist ihm durch Christum erkaufft.

Sanct Luke writtin in his ascention,
  Thocht present aye with vs hee bee,
The Scripture makis mention,
  That is to say with vs is hee,
Be his sweit word steidfast but faill,
Contraire the quhilk can not preuaill
  Sathan nor hellis tyranie.

Lucas thut gar schon schreiben
von seiner himmelfahrt
Doch allweg bey uns bleiben,
wie er versprochen hat,
  Vernimm : durch sein Gottliches wort;
wider das kann nicht siegen
kein gewalt der hellen pfort.

Ane comfortour to vs hee did send,
  Quhilke from the Father did proceide,
To gyde vs trewly to the end,
  In inwart thocht and outwart deid,
Call on the Lord, our gyde and licht,
To leid vs in his law full richt,
And be our helpe in all our neid.

Ein tröster thät er senden
das war der heilig Geist,
Von Gott thät er sie lenden
in wahrheit allermeist.
  Denselben wollen wir ruffen an,
der wird uns nicht verlassen
und uns treulich beystahn.

Pray for all men in generall,
  Suppose they wirk vs richt or wrang;
Pray for our prince in speciall;
  Thocht they be just, or tyrans strang,
Obey, for sa it aucht to bee.
In presoun for the veritie,
  Ane faythfull brother made this sang.

Recht lasst uns alle bitten
Christum für Obrigkeit
Ob wir schon von ihn litten
gewalt, auch für alle feind,
  Dass ihn Gott woll genedig sein :
hat Heinrich Müller gesungen
in dem gefängniss sein.'

ANE SANG OF THE EVANGELL, CON-
TEINAND THE EFFECT OF THE SAMINE.

EIN DANKLIED, FUR DIE HÖCHSTEN WOHL-
THATEN SO UNS GOTT IN CHRISTO
ERZEIGT HAT.

Bee blyth, all Christin men, and sing,
Dance and make myrth with all your
  micht,
Christ hes vs kythit greit comforting,
Quhairfoir wee may rejoyce of richt;
Ane warke to wonder that is wrocht,
Christ with his blud full deir vs bocht,
And for our saik to deid was dicht.

Nun freut euch, lieben Christen g'mein
und lasst uns frölich springen,
Dass wir getrost und all in ein
mit lust und liebe singen :
  Was Gott an uns gewendet hat,
und seine süsse wunderthat,
gar theur hat er's erworben.

For with the deuill and dulefull deid,
With hell and sinne I was forlorne,

Dem teufel ich gefangen lag,
im tod war ich verloren,

---

* As stated in this last verse, Henry Müller was the author of this hymn, and composed it while in
prison. His name is left out in the Scotch version, and Sir J. Dalyell seems to have supposed the reference
in it was to the imprisonment of the Scottish poet. The German appears first in the Magdeburg
Hymn-book of 1540.

The sonne of ire at God's feid,
Consauit sa I was and borne;
I grew ay mair and mair tharin,
And dayly eikit sinne to sinne,
Dispair was euer mee beforne.

Quhair I culd not the law fulfill,
My warkis made mee na supplie,
Sa blynd and waike was my freewill,
That hated the veritie;
My conscience kest mee euer in cair,
The diuell he draue mee in dispair,
And hell was euer befoir my eye.

God had greit pitie on my woe,
And above measure schew mee grace;
Quhen I was zet his cruell fo,
Yet he wald cure my carefull cace;
His lufe to mee hee did conuert,
From the maist deipest of his heart,
Quhilke cost him deare to make my peace.

To his beluffit Sonne hee said,
The tyme of mercie draweth neir,
To saif man and the diuell inuade:
Thairfoir, my hertlie Sonne so deir,
Goe fetch them from the feindis feid;
Thou man ouerthraw sinne, hell, and deid,
Syne man restoir baith hell and feir.

The Sonne his Father did obey,
And came down to the eird to mee,
Borne of ane maide, as wrytis Esay,
My kynd sweit brother for to bee;
Hee tuke on him my vilde nature,
And did his power foir to exile
Sathan and all his subtiltie.

Mein sünd mich quälte nacht und tag,
darin ich war geboren,
Ich fiel auch immer tiefer d'rein,
es war kein gut's am leben mein,
die sünd hatt mich besessen.

Mein gute werk die golten nicht,
es war mit ihn verdorben;
Der frei will hasset Gott's gericht,
er war zum gut erstorben;
Die angst mich zu verzweifeln trieb,
dass nichts denn sterben bei mir blieb,
zur höllen musst ich sinken.

Da jammerts Gott in ewigkeit
mein elend über massen,
Er dacht an sein barmherzigkeit,
er wollt mir helfen lassen,
Er wandt zu mir das vaterherz,
es war bei ihm fürwar kein scherz,
er liess sein bestes kosten.

Er sprach zu seinem lieben Sohn:
die zeit ist hie zu'rbarmen,
Fahr hin, mein's herzens werthe kron,
und sei das heil dem armen,
Und hilf ihm aus der sünden noth
erwürg für ihn den bittern tod
und lass ihn mit dir leben

Der Sohn dem Vater g'horsam ward,
er kam zu mir auf erden,
Von einer jungfrau rein und zart,
er sollt mein bruder werden.
Gar heimlich führt er sein gewalt,
er gieng in meiner armen g'stalt,
den teufel wollt er fangen.

Hee said, Thow sall haue victorie,
Gif thow allone on mee depend ;
For I will giue my selfe to thee,
That cairfull querrell to defend ;
For I am thine, and mine thow art,
And of my gloir thow sall haue part,
Syne ring with mee withouttin end.

Er sprach zu mir : halt dich an mich,
es soll dir jetzt gelingen.
Ich geb mich selber ganz für dich,
da will ich für dich ringen,
   Denn ich bin dein und du bist mein,
und wo ich bleib da sollst du sein,
uns soll der feind nicht scheiden.

They man sched out my blessit blude,
And raif alswa my lyfe fra mee ;
I thole this onely for thy gude,
Belieue that firm and stedfastlie :
For my deid sall thy deid deuoir,
That sinne sall thee condampne no moir,
For be that way saif thou man bee.

Vergiessen wird er mir mein blut,
dazu mein leben rauben :
Das leid ich alles dir zu gut,
das halt mit festem glauben.
   Den tod verschlingt das leben mein,
mein unschuld trägt die sünde dein,
da bist du selig worden.

Syne fra this present life I fare
To my Father celestiall :
Thy Mediatour trew sall bee there,
And send to thee my Spirit I sall,
To giue thee consolatioun,
In all thy tribulatioun :
The trueth hee sall instruct yow all.

Gen himmel zu dem vater mein
fahr ich von diesem leben,
Da will ich sein der meister dein,
den geist will ich dir geben,
   Der dich in trubniss trösten soll
und lehren mich erkennen wohl
und in der wahrheit leiten.

My doing, leirning mair and lesse,
That leir and doe vnfeinzeitlie ;
For that does God's kirk incres,
And his greit gloir dois magnifie.
Beware of men and their command,
Quhilk mee and my word doe gainstand,
My last will heir I leue to thee.

Was ich gethan hab und gelehrt
das sollst du thun und lehren,
Damit das reich Gott's werd gemehrt,
zu lob und seinen ehren,
   Und hüt dich für der menschen g'satz,
davon verdirbt der edle schatz,
das lass ich dir zu letze.*

* This is the first Hymn published by Luther in 1524. It appears in the Strassburg Hymn-books by 1537. Translations of it have been given by Miss Winkworth, and in the Sunday Magazine. The following is the first stanza of the latter version :

Dear Christians let us now rejoice,
   And dance in joyous measure :
All with one comfort and one voice,
   Singing in love and pleasure,

Of what for us our God hath done,
   The welcome wonder he hath shewn :
   Full dearly hath he bought it.

THE GREIT LOUING AND BLYTHNESSE OF
        GOD'S WORD.

VOM EVANGELISCHEN GLAUBEN.

Lord God, thy face and word of grace
Hes lang beene hid by craft of man,
Quhill at the last the nicht is past,
And wee full weill their falset ken.
Wee knaw perfyte the haly writ.
Therefore bee gloir and praise to thee,
Quhilke did vs giue this tyme to liue
Thy word trew preichit for to see.

. . . .

Sen, throw thy strenth, thy word at lenth,
Is preichit cleir before our eine,
Bee zit, gude Lord, misericord
To them quhilk yet dissauit beine,
And not dois knaw bot mens law,
To their great damnatioun;
Teich them fra hand to vnderstand
Thy word to their saluatioun.

Quha wald be saif, first this man haif,
To knaw their sin, syne trow in Christ:
Big on this ground, let lufe abound,
With patience, prayer, hope, and trust.
On God thou call, thanke him of all,
To serue thy neighbour giue thy cure.
Thy conscience free mone euer bee.
This can giue thee no creature.

O Herre Gott, dein Göttlich wort
ist lang verdunkelt blieben,
Bis durch dein' gnad' uns ist gesagt,
was Paulus hat geschrieben
    Und andere Apostel mehr,
aus dei'm Göttlichen munde:
Dess dancken dir mit fleiss, dass wir
erlebet ha'n die stunde.

Dass es mit macht an tag ist bracht,
wie klärlich ist für augen;
Ach Gott, mein Herr, erbarm dich der,
die dich noch ietzt verleugnen,
    Und achten sehr auff menschen lehr,
darin sie doch verderben:
Dein's wort's verstand mach ihn bekandt,
dass sie nicht ewig sterben.

Willst du nun fein gut Christen sein,
so musst du erstlich glauben:
Setz dein vertraun, darauff fest bau,
hoffnung und lieb im glauben
    Allein durch Christ zu aller frist,
dein nächsten lieb darneben,
Das g'wissen frey, rein hertz dabey,
das kein creatur kann geben.[*]

———   ———

I CALL ON THE, LORD.

EIN GEISTLICH LIED, ZU BITTEN VM
    GLAUBEN, LIEB VND HOFFNUNG.

I call on thee, Lord Jesus Christ,
I haue none other helpe but thee,

Ich ruff zu dir, Herr Jesu Christ,
ich bitt, erhor mein klagen;

[*] This hymn is ascribed by some to Speratus. It appears in the Strassburg book of 1537.

K

My hert is neuer set all at rest,
Till thy sweit word comfort mee.
Ane stedfast fayth grant mee therefore,
To hald be thy word euermore,
Aboue all thing euer resisting,
But to incres in fayth more and more.

Verleyh mir gnad zu dieser frist,
lass mich doch nicht verzagen.
 Den rechten weg, O Herr, ich mein,
den wollest du mir geben,
dir zu leben,
mei'm nächsten nütz sein,
dein wort zu halten eben.

Yet anes againe I call to thee,
Heir my requeist, O mercifull Lord ;
I wald faine hope in thy mercie,
And can not bee thereto restorde,
Except thou illuminate with thy grace,
My blind and naturall waiknesse :
Cause mee therefore haue hope in store,
In thy mercie and sweit promise.

Ich bitt noch mehr, O Herre Gott,
du kannst es mir wohl geben :
Das ich nicht wieder werd zu spott,
die hoffnung gib darneben ;
 Voraus, wenn ich muss hie davon,
dass ich dir mög vertrauen,
und nicht bauen
auff alles mein thun,
sonst wirds mich ewig reuen.

Lord, print into my heart and mynde,
Thy Haly Spirit with feruentnesse,
That I to thee bee not vnkinde,
Bot loue thee without fenzeitnesse.
Let nothing draw my mynde from thee,
But euer to loue thee earnestly;
Let not my hert vnkindly depart,
From the richt loue of thy mercie.

Verleyh, das ich aus hertzens grund
mein feinden mög vergeben,
Verzeih mir auch zu dieser stund,
schaff mir ein neues leben.
 Dein wort mein speis lass allweg sein,
damit mein seel zu nähren,
mich zu wehren,
wenn vnglück geht daher,
das mich bald möcht verkehren.

Giue mee thy grace, Lord, I thee pray,
To loue my enemies heartfullie,
Howbeit they trouble mee alway,
And for thy cause doe sclander mee.
Zet Jesus Christ, for thy goodnesse,
Fulfill my hert with forgiuenesse ;
That whill I leif, I them forgeif,
That doe offend mee moir and lesse.

Lass mich kein lust noch furcht von dir
in dieser welt abwenden,
Beständig sein ins end gib mir,
du hast allein in händen,
 Und wem du's gibst, der hat's umsonst,
es mag niemand erwerben
noch ererben
durch werk dein gnad,
die uns errett't vom sterben.

I am compassit round about,
With sore and strang temptatioun,
Therfor, gude Lord, delyuer mee out
From all this wicked natioun.
'The deuill, the warld, the flesh also,
Dois follow mee where euer I goe :
Therefore wald I delyuerit bee,
Thy helpe I seeke, Lord, and no mo.

Ich lieg im streit und widerstreb,
hilff, O Herr Christ, dem schwachen,
An deiner gnad allein ich kleb,
du kannst mich starker machen.
  Kommt nun anfechtung her, so wehr,
dass sie mich nicht umstosse,
du kannst massen,
dass mirs nicht bringt gefähr,
ich weis, du wirst's nicht lassen.

Now seis thow, Lord, what neid I haue,
There is no vther to pleinzie to :
Therefore thy Haly Gaist I craife,
To bee my gyde where euer I goe,
That in all my aduersitie ;
I forzet not the loue of thee ;
Bot as thou, Lord, hes giuen thy word,
Let mee therein both leue and die.

QUARE FREMUERUNT GENTES.—Psalm ii.

Quhat is the cause, God omnipotent,
  That all natiouns commufit are so sore ?
The kinges and the people with ane consent,
  Resistés thee, thy power and glore.
  They stryve against thy law aye more
      and more,   [hes send
And contrair Christ thy Son whom thou
To save all men that will on him depend.

Hilff Gott, wie geht das immer zu
  Dass alles volck so grimmet ?
Fürsten und konig all gemein,
  mit eins sind sie gesinnet :
Wider zu streben deiner hand,
und Christo, den du hast gesandt,
  der gantzen welt zu helffen.

They will not bee reformed from their sinne,
  But will remaine blindit in ignorance,
And will not thole to luke thy law within,
  But castis it away with greit grevance,

Sie wöllen ungestraffet sein
  und leben nach ihr'm sinne,
Und werffen von sich deinen rath,
  und was du lehrest d'rinne,

---

* The German Hymn is by Speratus, and it is said to have been inserted in the Strassburg Hymn books as early as 1537.

Thy counsell they refusit and governance, Sie gehen nach ihres hertzen wahn,
And following their owne heartes consait, ein iedermann auff seiner bahn,
Everie man drawes a sindrie gait. und lassen ihn nicht wehren.

But thou, O God, in heavin into thy ring, Du aber in dem hymmel hoch,
  Thou makes* all their counsellis everi-   O Gott wirst sie belachen,
    eich one   [bring Verspotten ihren besten rath
What they intend that sall they never und †ihrn anschlag verachten,
  To finall end ; for thy wisedome alone, Du wirst mit zorn sie sprechen an
  Their pregnant wittes sall scorne and und straffen was sie ha'n gethan
    anone,   mit grimm wirst du sie schrecken.
In thy great ire thou sall them sair reprufe,
And from thy face thou sall them swyth
  remufe.

For God has set ane Captaine starke and Der Herr hat zum könig gesetzt
  wight,   [naturall,   Christum, den ihr verkleinet,
  Christ his owne Sonne, God and man Auf Zion seinen heiligen berg,
On Mont Sinay to rule it just and right,   das ist uber sein gemeine,
  That is to say, God's kirk universall, Dass er soll kund thun überall,
  To teach his Father's word celestiall : des Vaters sinn und wohlgefall
His godly will and pleasour for to shaw, und lehren sein gesetze.
Instructing all the warld into his law.

God said to him, Thou art my Sonne and Er sprach zu ihm du bist mein Sohn
  I thee begat for ever, and this day, [air, heut hab ich dich gezelet, ‡
Thy deid purchest victorie preclare, Von dem tode erwecket schon,
  Syne from the deid thou raise to ring und in dir auserwählet
    for aye.   [cay. Für erben and für kinder mein,
  My chosen in thee sall not come to de- die gläuben an den namen dein,
Quha trowly trustes in thy godly name dass sie all' durch dich leben.
Sall never die eternally I plaine.

My Sonne, I will thee give all nations Die heiden will ich schencken dir,
  In heritage, and put them in thy cure, mein kind, zu einem erbe,
To rule them with thy ministratiouns, Dass du mit deinem wort in ihn,

* Query makes for mockest.   † Another edition has here "ihn zu nichte machen."
‡ Edition 1533 has here "geboren," and in line 4 "ausserkoren."

And priefe them with thy croce at thy
  plesour.   [them pure,
To purge their fleshly lust and make
And for to raise their mindes spirituall,
To prayse thy name now and perpetuall.

des fleisches lust verderbest;
Ein neu volck sollst du richten an,
das meinen namen preisen kann
  an allem ort auff erden

Heirfoir, kings and rewlers, now bewar,
  Advert till God's word and discipline;
Receve his Sonne; above all things, prefar
  His godly word, and keipe well his
    doctrine: [syne.
  Learn him to dreid and traist intill him
Whilk is the trew wirship and righteousnes,
That God requires of mankind mair and
  les.

Darum, ihr konig, mercket nun;
  ihr sollt euch lassen lehren,
Und diesem konig horen zu,
  sein wort halten in ehren.
Dass ihr Gott lernet furchten wohl,
und wie ein hertz ihm trauen soll,
  das heisst recht, Gott wohl dienen.

Resaif therefoir his sweit correctioun,
  That he na mair with zow offendit be,
Befoir your eine with trew affectioun,
  And in zour hart ze have him idently.
Obey his law for when grevit is he,
Then wha daur his just judgement abide,
Blissit are they whilk on him doth confide.

Nehmt auff die straff williglich,
  dass nicht erzorn der Herre,
Halt ihn fur augen statiglich,
  und lebt nach seiner lehre.
Wenn sein zorn als ein feuer auffgeht,
wohl ist dem, der fur ihm besteht,
  das sind, die auff ihn trauen.*

For part of Psalm XII., see pp. 52, 53.

USQUE QUO DOMINE—PSALM xiii.

O Lord how long for ever will thou for-
  get?   [lang
And hyde thy face fra me, or zet how
Sall I reheirs thy counsell in my hert?
  When sall my hert ceis of this sorie
  sang?

Ach Gott, wie lang vergissest mein
  gar noch bis an das ende!
Ach Gott wie lang das antlitz dein
  Thust du doch von mir wenden!
Wie lang soll ich selbs rathen mir,
  In meiner seel ein schmerz gebir
  Den gantzen tag im hertzen.

* This version of Psalm II. is said to be by Andreas Knopken, and to have appeared in the Enchiridion of 1528. It is found in the Magdeburg and in the Strassburg Hymn-books.

[Mine enemie exalted be how lang?]   Wie lang wird doch mein feind erhöcht?
O Lord, behald, help me, and light my eine   Sieh, Gott, thu mich erhören!
That sudden sleep of death do me na teine.   Erleucht auch meine augen recht,
                                              Und thu mich herr gewehren,
Or els when my enemies sees my fall,   Dass ich nicht in dem todt entschlaff
   Wee did prevaill, soon will they say on   Und dass mein feind nicht arges schaff,
   mee   Sprech, hab mich uberwunden.
And gif they see me brought in thrall,
   They will rejoyce into their tyrannie.   Und ob ich viel in sünd und leid
   Bot I in God hes hope, and trust to see   Mein feind wurdt sich erspringen.
His godly helpe; then sall I love the Lord, Ich hoff in dein barmhertzigkeit,
Whilk did me save from them that had   Dem herren will ich singen.
   me schord.*   Mein hertz freut sich in deinem heil
                                        Der mich begab mit gutem Theil,
                                        Sein namen will ich preisen.

DOMINE QUIS HABITABIT.——PSALM XV.†

O Lord quha sall in heaven dwell,   O Herr, wer wird wohnunge hon
   In thy triumphant throne and tabernacle?   in deinen zelten kluge,
Or quha sall on thy halie hill sa hie,   Auff deinem heilgen berge schon
   Make residence and have his habitacle?   da ewig ha'n sein ruge?
The innocent that is ane spectakill   Der unbefleckten wandel trei't,
Of holy life and conversatioun,   Und wirket die gerechtigkeit
And just in all his operatioun.   wahrhaftig in sei'm hertzen.

  .   .   .   .

---

  * The Scotch version of this Psalm, without the line supplied in brackets, would consist of thirteen
lines—a form of stanza never elsewhere found in this writer, but with the addition of that line we get
two of the seven-lined stanzas so common in his book, and these two stanzas embrace all that is contained in the three of the German hymn.
  † The stanza in the Scotch and German is the same, and the general resemblance in meaning is
pretty close, and yet one can hardly doubt that the Scotch poet had also Marôt's French version of the
psalm, and took the words "tabernacle" and "habitacle" from it though there is no marked resemblance
between the two in other respects.

DOMINUS ME REGIT, Psa. xxiii.

The Lord God is my Pastour gude,
  Aboundantly mee for to feid ;
Then how can I bee destitute
  Of any gude thing in my neid ?
Hee feid me in feildes faire,
To riuers sweit, pure and preclair,
Hee dryues mee bot ony dreid.

Der Herr Gott ist mein treuer hirt
  Halt mich in seiner hute,
Darinn mir gar nicht mangeln wird
  Yendert an einem gute.
Er weidet mich ohn unterlass,
  Da aufwächst das wohlschmecket grass
Seines heilsamen wortes.

My saull and lyfe hee dois refresh,
And mee conuoyes in the way
Of his justice and righteousnesse,
And mee defends from decay.
Not for my warkes verteousnesse,
But for his name so glorious,
Preserues mee baith night and day.

Zum reinen wasser er mich weist
  Das mich erquicken thutte
Das ist sein frohnheiliger geist
  Der mich macht wohlgemuthe,
Er führet mich auf rechter strass
In sein'n geboten ohn ablass
  Von wegen seines namens.

And though I wander, or goe will,
  Or am in danger for to die,
No dreid of deid sall cum me till,
  Nor fear of cruell tyrannie :
Because that thou art mee beside,
To gouerne me and be my gyde
From all mischief and miserie.

Ob ich wandert im finstern thal
  furcht ich kein ungelücke
In verfolgung leiden, trübsal
  und dieser welte tücke,
Wann du bist bei mir stätiglich,
dein stab und stecken trösten mich
  auf dein wort ich mich lasse.

And thow ane tabill does prouyde
Before mee, full of all delyte,
Contrair to my perseuars pryde,
To their displeasure and dispyte.
Thou hes annoynted my head,
And full my cup thou hes made,
With many dishes of delyte.

Du bereitest vor mich ein tisch
  für mein feind allenthalben,
Machst mein hertz unverzagt frisch,
  Mein haupt thust du mir salben.
Mit deinem geist, der freuden öl,
und schenkest voll ein meiner seel
  deiner geistlichen freuden.

Thy gudnesse and benignity,
Let euer bee with mee therefore;
And while I liue, vntill I die,
Thou lay them vp with mee in store;
That I may haue my dwelling place
Into thy house, before thy face,
To ring with thee for euermore.

Gutes und die barmhertzigkeit
laufen mir nach im leben,
Und ich werd bleiben allezeit,
im haus des Herren eben,
Auf erd in der Christlichen g'mein,
Und nach dem tode werd ich sein
bei Christo meinem Herren.

IV.

When, in the spring of 1861, it fell to my lot to give the closing address to your Association, I thought it my duty to take as my subject "the Scottish Reformation and the Constitution of the Reformed Church of Scotland," as it appeared to me only seemly that, in an institution which had been so closely connected with the fortunes of the Reformed Church, the session should not be allowed to terminate without some special reference to that event which had just before been so generally commemorated throughout the country. I took advantage of that opportunity to give a succinct account of the connection of our University and its alumni with the great movement which was so successfully brought to an issue in 1560, and which has been the source of untold blessings to our native land; and after describing the doctrine, worship, discipline, and government of our Church as then established, I enforced the practical duty of our holding fast by the great doctrines which we have received in common with the other Churches of the Reformation, and endeavouring to cultivate the same friendly intercourse with these as our fathers did. In the circumstances, I could hardly pass without notice an address which had been given some time before in our city, and in which, while our Reformer and his work had been spoken of with far more kindness and respect than Mr Lyon was wont to show, it seemed yet to be hinted that it was from disappointment and embitterment of spirit

—almost from jealousy or from feelings of wounded vanity, on account of the treatment he had received at the hands of the English Reformers and exiles, that he made the constitution of the Scottish Church so different from the Elizabethan, and did not use his great influence to bring about a closer uniformity between them. The answer I ventured to give to this implied censure was, that in acting as he did, and making the constitution of the Church what he made it, Knox only followed out the opinions on this subject which rightly or wrongly were entertained by the ablest scholars and divines of his day, and which, in so far as they were left at liberty to do so, they also followed out, and which many in England itself would, at least in part, have carried out had they been allowed by the civil power to do so. Mr Froude, in the two volumes of his history since published, has supplied a farther vindication of our Reformer from the censure passed on him, by showing that had he been at all inclined to be affected by such slights, he met with more than enough in the earlier years of Elizabeth's reign to have alienated him for ever from her and her ministers; but, with the undaunted resolution of a true patriot, he bore all patiently, and labouring on in concert with them, saved Elizabeth's throne and Protestant ascendancy in Britain in spite of her waywardness, unkindness, and inconsistency. And he and Mr Carlyle, by their recent addresses in Edinburgh, rendered good service to our National Church by bearing so emphatic testimony to the uprightness and patriotism of Knox just at the time when some were beginning to doubt whether the representation of his character made by Dr M'Crie was not far too favourable. I do not mean, on the present occasion, to enter at any length into this controverted question, but wish simply and briefly, before passing to my proper subject, to state that subsequent research has supplied me with a farther answer to these charges against our Reformer, which, if more were really needed, should refute them utterly. Among the many works prepared by the divines of the sixteenth century which, after having been long as good as lost, have been once more brought to light in our day, are those of John a Lasco, which have just been republished in Holland. Respecting the author, I need only tell you at present that he was a Pole of noble birth, who had embraced the

L

Reformed faith, and who, after various fortunes, was, with other foreigners in trouble for their religion, invited to settle in England early in the reign of Edward VI.   With the approbation of the king, he was made super-intendent of the German and other foreign churches in London, and was allowed, after a time, to draw up for the churches under his superinten-dence forms of worship and discipline which in all essential respects closely resembled those which, under the guidance of Knox, the Church of Scotland afterwards adopted.   In the ordinary forms for public worship, indeed, and also in the forms for the administration of the sacraments and of marriage, any verbal coincidences that occur are rather with the offices of Calvin and Pollanus than with those of a Lasco, yet, even in these, prayers are occasionally inserted at places in which they are found in a Lasco's formulary, and are not found in Calvin's, and in such things as the posture of the communicants and their arrangement at the communion table, the influence of a Lasco is plainly traceable.   Then the description of the respective duties of superintendents, ministers, elders and deacons, are closely similar in a Lasco's book, and in the First Book of Discipline, and while I doubt if even the explicit statement in the former respecting the permanence of the superintendent's office will suffice to explain away what is said in the latter to an apparently opposite effect, I can have no doubt that the equally explicit statements of the former book, as to the limitations of the superintendent's powers, and his liability to be removed by the ordinary ministers of the church, should occasion call for it, must cast additional light on the similar statements of the latter book, and tend to remove any lingering hesitation any may still feel in coming to the conclusion that these superintendents were very different from diocesan bishops.   Moreover, the form and order for the election and admission of superintendents and ministers, and the order of excommunication and public repentance "set furth be Mr John Knox," coincide remarkably throughout both in general structure and in language with those of a Lasco, so that there can be no question that the one is derived from the other.   A Lasco's "Forma ac ratio tota ecclesiastici ministerii in peregri-norum ecclesia institutâ Londini" was drawn up in England during the life of Edward VI., but was only published after his death, when its author with his flock was again banished the kingdom, and was for a time settled in Frankfort. This, so far as I can ascertain, happened in the very year that Knox's friends were there, and the circumstances in which the book originated could hardly fail to be known to those of the English congregation who were contending earnestly for farther reformation in worship. These circumstances are fully detailed in the epistle dedicatory to his kinsman the King of Poland, which a Lasco prefixed to his book. In it he expressly asserts that as England was not then deemed ripe for a complete reformation, he was instructed by the king to draw up the constitution of the church of the foreigners in strict accordance with the regulations of scripture, and without regard to human rites, however ancient and venerable, that when the day should come when the nation would bear a more thorough reformation, it might have, in the practice of these foreign churches, a reliable directory which it could follow. In all this a Lasco states that the king was supported by most of his Council, and especially by that wise counsellor and earnest reformer, Thomas Cranmer, Archbishop of Canterbury. What was more natural then that the English congregation at Geneva should have a liking for a Lasco's forms, and that when Knox, on his return to Britain, was met with the old bugbear, "England is not yet ripe for such a reformation as you want," he should reply, "Well, we will take things just as they were allowed to be set down by your best men in the time of the good King Edward, and when you are disposed to advance to that perfection which he and his advisers so earnestly desired for you, you will know where to find us." What better proof could he have given that he was superior to such petty motives as have been imputed to him, and was every inch a true patriot.

The following is the passage from a Lasco's epistle dedicatory to which reference is made above:—

Hæc ergo nobis etiam consilii nostri ratio fuit in restituendis cultus divini ritibus totáque adeo ministerii instauratione, posteaquam divino beneficio Ecclesiam nobis per pientissimum Principem atque æternâ dignum memoriâ, Eduardum, eius nomini sextum, Angliæ etc. Regem, concessam haberemus. Cupiebat Rex ille Sanctissimu ita restitutam, quoad eius fieri posset, in universo regno suo omnem plane religionem, ut nullâ fere aliâ de re pro ætate suâ sollicitus magis esset. Adhibebat in ejus rei consilium, quos pietate eruditione ac judicio aliis antecellere intelligebat, inter quos præcipuum habebat Thomam Cranmerum, Cantuariensem Archiepiscopum, virum, præter insignem eruditionem ac pietatem, eâ quoque ingenii dexteritate prudentiâ ac morum gravitate præditum (quæ interim summam comitatem ac modestiam conjunctam habebat), ut hæc omnia simul in illo sine magnâ profecto admiratione nemo facile intueri posset. Hujus igitur hortatu cum ego quoque per Regem illum vocatus essem et leges quædam patriæ obstarent, quominus publici potissimum cultus divini ritus, sub Papismo usurpati, pro eo ac Rex ipse cupiebat, repurgari protinus possent—ego vero pro Peregrinorum Ecclesiis sedulo instarem—ita demum placuit ut ritus publici in Anglicis Ecclesiis per gradus quosdam, quantum per leges patriæ omnino liceret, repurgarentur : Peregrinis vero hominibus, qui patriis hâc alioqui in parte legibus non usque adeo tenerentur, Ecclesiæ concederentur, in quibus omnia libere et nullâ rituum patriorum habitâ ratione, juxta doctrinam duntaxat atque observationem Apostolicam instituerentur; ita enim fore, ut Anglicæ quoque Ecclesiæ ad puritatem Apostolicam amplectendam unanimi omnium regni ordinum consensu excitarentur. Ejus vero consilii Rex ipsemet pro suâ pietate præcipuus non autor tantum, sed etiam propugnator fuit. Etsi enim id in Senatu Regio omnibus propemodum placeret, *ipseque Cantuariensis Archiepiscopus rem modis omnibus promoveret*, non deerat tamen, qui id moleste ferrent adeoque et reluctaturi fuerint huic instituto regio, nisi Rex ipse, non tantum auctoritate suâ restitisset, sed productis etiam instituti hujus rationibus conatus eorum repressisset.

A Lasco, while in England, had pronounced himself decidedly favourable to the wishes of Hooper and the Puritans, and I daresay the above will be thought to confirm certain statements made by them respecting the personal opinions of Cranmer.

I subjoin to this a few extracts from a Lasco's "Forma inaugurandi Ministros verbi et Superintendentem ad ministerium ipsorum," and "Knox's Form and Order of election and admission" of superintendents and ministers, merely premising that the formularies are pretty similar throughout, and not merely in the parts I select :

PRECATIO SUPER ELECTIS VERBI MINIS-   THE PRAYER.
TRIS CIRCA IPSORUM INAUGURATIONEM.

"Domine Deus, fili Dei vivi, Jesu   O Lord, to whom all Power is gevin
Christe' qui te Ecclesiæ tuæ ad finem   in Heavin and in Earth, thou that art the

usque sæculi semper adfuturum esse pro-
misisti, ut illam regas ac gubernes Spiritu
sancto tuo, quique illam ita diligis, ut
non solum sanguinem tuum innocentissi-
mum pro ea semel fuderis, sed huius
quoque tanti tui beneficii testes ac doc-
tores in illa perpetuo extare velis ad in-
staurationem sanctorum et consumma-
tionem absolvendam in mystico tuo
(quod nos sumus) corpore.—Te jam
supplices deprecamur, Domine Rex,
Doctor ac Pontifex noster æterne! ut
hosce viros fratres nostros (si plures sint
electi ad ministerium), per nos ad verbi
ministerium in tuo sancto nomine electos,
spiritu sancto tuo replere digneris, ut
verbi tui divini ministerium beneficior-
umque tuorum salutare atque efficax
testimonium inter nos retineatur et con-
servetur. Largire illis Domine! pruden-
tiam recte secandi verbum tuum. Da ut
Satanæ et Antichristi dolos ac tyranni-
dem ab Ecclesiâ hâc nostra fideliter ac
diligenter arceant, eiusque reliquias
omnes, si quæ adhuc inter nos haerent,
prorsus extirpent ac propellant. Dona
illis Domine! eiusmodi os et sapientiam,
ut ora omnium adversiorum verbi tui
auctoritate obturare luposque a grege tuo
abigere possint, quo ita demum populus
hic tuus, per ipsorum ministerium in
verâ tui cognitione instructus, te laudare,
tibi gratias agere inque voluntatis tuæ
sanctæ obedientiâ et omni pietate indies
magis ac magis promovere possit, ad
regni tui Patrisque tui coelestis gloriam
immortalem, quem etiam per tuum

the eternal Sone of the eternall Father,
who hast not onlie so loved thy Church,
that for the Redemptioun and Purga-
tioun of the same, thou . . . hast
sched thy most innocent Blode . . .
bot also to retene this thy most ex-
cellent Benefit in recent Memorie, hast
appointed in thy Church Teachers, Pas-
tors and Apostels, to instruct, confort
and admonish the same: Look upon us
mercifully, O Lord, thou that only art
King, Teacher and hie Preast to thy
awin Flock: And send unto this our
Brother, whom in thy Name we have
charged with the cheif cair of thy Church
within the Boundis of Louthian, such
portion of thy holy Spirit, as thereby he
may rightlie divyd thy Word to the In-
structioun of thy Flock, and to the Con-
futatioun of pernitious Erroris and dam-
nable Superstitiouns: Geve unto him,
good Lord, a Mouth and Wisedom,
whereby the Enemies of thy Trueth may
be confounded, the Wolfes expelled and
drevin from thy Fald, thy Schep may be
fed in the holesome Pastures of thy most
holy Word, the blind and ignorant may
be illuminated with thy trew knowledge.
Finallie, that the Dregges of Superstit-
tion and Idolatrie, which yet resteth
within this Realme, being purged and removed, we may all not only have Occasion to glorifie thee our only Lord and
Saviour, bot also daylie to grow in God-
lines and Obedience of thy most holy
will. . . . by Participation of thy holy
Spirit, which by trew Faith in thee, we

nomen, ut abs te edocti sumus, supplices invocamus, dicentes : Pater noster etc."

Finitâ precatione, accedunt ad electos Ministros, alii ministri et Seniores Ecclesiæ omnes, et capitibus illorum manus unâ omnes imponunt, quibus etiam assistens Ecclesiastes, et manus unâ cum illis capitibus electorem imponens, clarâ voce, auscultante totâ Ecclesiâ, dicit :

do profes as the blessed of thy Father, of whom the perpetuall Encrease of thy Graces we crave, as by thee our Lord, King, and onlie Bischop we ar taught to pray, Our Father, &c.

The Prayer ended, the rest of the Ministers and Eldars of that Church, if any be present, in Signe of there consent shall tak the elected be the hand.

The chiefe Minister shall give the Benedictioun as followeth :

THE BENEDICTIOUN.

" Deus et Pater noster coelestis, qui vos ad verbi sui Ministerium in hâc suâ Ecclesia vocavit, illuminet vos spiritu sancto suo suâque manu potenti vos corroboret et vestrum ministerium ita regat et gubernet, ut in illo fideliter et cum fructu versari semper possitis, ad propagandum regnum unigeniti sui filii in Ecclesia ipsius per Evangelii sui institutam ab ipso prædicationem, propter eundem ipsum unigenitum suum filium, Jesum Christum, Dominum et servatorem nostrum. Amen."

God the Father of our Lord Jesus Christ, who. . . hath called thee to the Office of a Watch-man owir his People, multiplie his Graces with thee, illuminate thee with his holy Spirit, confort and strenthen thee in all Vertew, governe and guyde thy Ministerie to the Prayse of his holy Name, to the Propagation of Christ's Kingdome, to the Confort of his Church, and finally, to the plaine Discharge and Assurance of thy awin Conscience in the Day of the Lord Jesus ; to whom with the Father, and with the holy Ghost, be all Honour, Prayse and Glory, now and evir : So be it.

POSTREMA ADMONITIO AD INAUGURATOS VERBI MINISTROS, ANTEQUAM PSALMUS DECANTETUR.

Viri fratres! attendite vobis ipsis. . . .
Pascite concreditum vobis gregem Christi,

THE LAST EXHORTATION TO THE ELECTED.

Tak· Heed to thy selfe, and unto the Flock committed to thy charge, feid the

curam illius habete, non velut adacti, sed ultro ac sponte vestrâ, non turpis lucri studio, sed liberaliter, neque dominium vobis usurpantes in Ecclesiam, sed sitis velut exemplaria gregis. Rebus adversis (vobis alioqui semper expectandis) ne frangamini. Contemptum probra et convicia addictorum mundo hominum. . . . cum omni tolerantiâ sustinete, . . . proposito vobis exemplo Prophetarum atque Apostolorum omnium et ipsius denique Christi domini. Præstate vos fideles ac diligentes Christi Domini et spiritus sancti cooperarios in arguendo mundo de peccato, justitiâ et judicio ipsius. Ne efferamini animo, si quando vobis ex sententia aliquid succedat prosperenturve aliquo modo res vestræ, multo minus vero opes aut honores mundi huius expetatis. Consolemini afflictos, egenos sublevetis pro vestrâ virili atque alios ad id faciendum omni vestro studio exhortemini. . . . In hoc toti incumbite, ut studio ac conatu vestro plura alia talenta communi nostro omnium Domini per eius gratiam lucrifacere possitis. Ita fiet enim, ut, superatis tandem vestris laboribus omnibus, reportetis proculdubio, ubi Princeps ille pastorum omnium summus atque æternus apparuerit, coronam gloriæ immarcessibilem. . . . . Deus et Pater noster coelestis concedat per immensam suam misericordiam, ut omnes pariter vocem hanc olim audire possimus, propter filium suum dilectum, Dominum nostrum. Amen.

same cairfullie, not as it wer be Compulsion, bot of very Lufe, which thou bearest to the Lord Jesus, walke in Simplicitie and Purenes of Lyfe, as it becumeth the trew Servand and the Embassadour of the Lord Jesus. Usurpe not Dominion nor tyrannicall Authoritie owir thy Brethren : Be not discouraged in Adversitie, bot lay before thy self the example of the Prophets, Apostles, and of the Lord Jesus, who in thair ministery sustened contradiction, Contempt, Persecution, and Death : Feare not to rebuke the World of Sin, Justice and Judgment: If anything succeid prosperouslie in thy vocation, be not puft up with Pryde, neither yet flatter thy self, as that the good succes proceided from thy Vertew, Industrie, or Cair ; Bot let evir that Sentence of the Apostle remain in thy Hart, *What hast thou which thou hast not receaved? If thou hast receaved why glories thou?* Confort the Afflicted, support the Poore, and exhort utheris to support them : Be not solist for Things of this Lyfe, but be fervent in Prayer to God for the Increase of his holie Spirit. And finallie, behave thy self in this holy Vocation with such Sobriety as God may be glorified in thy Ministerie : And so shal thou schortly obteine the Victorie, and shal receave the Crowne promised, when the Lord Jesus shall appeare in his Glorie, whose omnipotent Spirit assist thee and us to the end. Amen.

The resemblance in the prayers and exhortations of a Lasco's " Ratio ac Forma publicæ pœnitentiae," and his " Modus ac Ritus excommunicationis," and those in Knox's order of excommunication and public repentance are quite as striking, though it is evident Knox's work is not a hasty copy but a carefully considered transcript in which the original is generally shortened and sometimes improved. To exhibit fully the correspondences between these treatises, however, would require me to extend this appendix beyond all reasonable length.   I subjoin a few brief extracts and headings from the part relating to public repentance :

Nemo ad publicam pœnitentiam prius admittitur, quam illius resipiscentia per Ministros ac Seniores Ecclesiæ in cœtu ipsorum djligenter exploretur. . . . .

It is first to be observed that none may be admitted to publique Repentance except that first they be admitted thereto by the Session and Assemblie of the Ministeris and Eldaris. . . .

Precatio super lapso et pœnitente, &c.

The prayer, &c.

Admonitio ad lapsum ac pœnitentem fratrem.

The prayer finished, the Minister shall turn him to the penitent Brother and in full audience shall say, . . .

Admonitio ad Ecclesiam.

Ane Admonition to the Church.

Gratiarum actio pro resipiscentia lapsi fratris.

The Thanksgiving.

Finita hac gratiarum actione quærit Minister a pœnitente fratre illo, num deinceps quoque disciplinæ ecclesiasticæ subesse velit juxta verbum Dei, illeque respondet: " Etiam."

Tum Minister illi annunciat et contestatur veram ac plenam peccati ipsius, coram Deo et ejus Ecclesia remissionem, &c. Postremo Ministri ac Seniores ordine omnes fratrem pœnitentem illum dextris datis amplexantur in totius Ecclesiæ conspectu, &c. Atque ita demum Psalmus gratulatorius canitur a tota Ecclesia (Psal. 103 aut alius similis),

The Thanksgiving being finished, the Minister shall require of the Penitent, if that he will be subject to the Discipline of the Church, in caise that he after offend ; who answering that he will, the Minister shall say in maner of Absolution : If thou unfainedly repentis, &c. Then shall the Eldaris and Deacons with Ministeris (if anie be) in the Name of the whole Church take the reconciled Brother by the Hand and embrace him in Signe of full Reconciliation. Then after shall the Church sing the ciii. Psalm. . . . .

www.ingramcontent.com/pod-product-compliance
Lightning Source LLC
Chambersburg PA
CBHW032248080426
42735CB00008B/1052